DRIVING STANDARDS AGENCY

D0279305

DRIVING SKILLS

THE COMPLETE
THEORY TEST
for Cars and
Motorcycles

including the questions and answers

London: HMSO

Written and compiled by the Publications Unit of the Driving
Standards Agency

Questions and answers compiled by the National Foundation
for Educational Research

Illustrations by Vicky Squires
Designed, edited and published by HMSO

© Crown copyright 1996
Applications for reproduction should be made to HMSO's
Copyright Unit, St. Clements House, 2-16 Colegate, Norwich, NR3 1BQ

Fifth impression 1996

ISBN 0 11 551779 0

British Library Cataloguing in Publication Data
A CIP catalogue record for this book is available from the
British Library

Acknowledgements

The Driving Standards Agency would like to thank the
following for their assistance:

National Foundation for Educational Research

Transport Research Laboratory

Department of Transport, Road Safety Division

Driver and Vehicle Testing Agency, Northern Ireland

The Staff of the Driving Standards Agency

DSA THEORY TEST for cars and motorcycles

DSA THEORY TEST for cars and motorcycles

The Driving Standards Agency (DSA) is an Executive Agency of the Department of Transport. You will see its logo at test centres.

The aim of the DSA is to promote road safety through the advancement of driving standards.

DSA

- Conducts practical driving tests for cars, motorcycles, lorries and other vehicles

- Plans, maintains and supervises the theory test for cars, motorcycles and lorries

- Controls the register of Approved Driving Instructors (ADIs)

- Supervises Compulsory Basic Training (CBT) courses for motorcyclists

- Aims to provide a high-quality service to its customers

DVTA

The Driver and Vehicle Testing Agency (DVTA) is an Executive Agency within the Department of the Environment for Northern Ireland. Its primary aim is to promote and improve road safety through the advancement of driving standards and implementation of the Government's policies for improving the mechanical standards of vehicles.

PART ONE   **Getting Started**

PART TWO   **The Question Paper**

PART THREE   **The Questions and Answers**

PART FOUR   **Conclusion**

CONTENTS

With the ever-increasing traffic on today's roads, it is important to make sure that new drivers have a broad spread of driving knowledge. This is recognised by the introduction of a separate theory test, which is a major step towards improving road safety in the United Kingdom (UK).

This book is intended to help new drivers prepare for the theory test. It will enable them to appreciate the depth of knowledge of driving theory which is required. A sound grounding in and extensive knowledge of driving theory will help toward a better understanding of practical driving skills. These are necessary to become a safe and confident driver.

This book contains the theory test question bank, set out in an easy-to-read style with lots of illustrations. To aid learning, this book explains why the answers are correct and identifies good driving practices.

There are other books in the driving skills series which will help you to develop your skills.

The Driving Manual
The Motorcycling Manual
The Driving Test

All are published by HMSO.

There is also a video entitled *Your Driving Test - the Video* (HMSO), which is designed to explain what to expect during the test and to dispel some of the myths associated with it. A fully interactive CD-ROM *The Theory Test and Beyond* (HMSO) is also available to help you to develop your knowledge in the most up-to-date way.

The Chief Driving Examiner
Driving Standards Agency

This book will help you to

▶ Study for your theory test
▶ Prepare and help you to pass

Part One will give you information on how to get started.

Part Two will tell you about the question paper and how to answer it.

Part Three will show you the questions that may be used on your test. Don't worry, you won't have to answer ALL of them. Your paper will have 35 questions.

The questions are in the left-hand column with the answers beneath. On the right of the page you will find a brief explanation of why the answer is correct.

Books for study

It is strongly recommended that you study a copy of *The Highway Code*. You can order one when you apply for your provisional licence or buy one from a good bookshop. The DSA publication *The Driving Manual* (HMSO) will explain driving skills in more detail, and *Know Your Traffic Signs* (HMSO) is highly recommended. These books are available from any good bookshop. Books are also available from other publishers.

Driving is a life skill.
Your tests are just the beginning.

The Driving Standards Agency thinks it is important you study – not just to pass the test but to become a safe driver.

DSA THEORY TEST for cars and motorcycles

Applying for your licence

You will need to apply for a provisional licence.

An application form (D.1) can be obtained from a post office.

When you receive your licence sign it immediately. Don't drive until you have done so.

You can't take your theory test until you have your provisional licence. You will have to take it with you when you take your test.

If you want to drive a car

The Driving Standards Agency (DSA) approves instructors to teach learner drivers for payment.

These instructors have their standards checked regularly.

Approved Driving Instructors must

- Pass a difficult exam
- Reach a high standard of instruction
- Be registered with the DSA or the DVTA
- Display an Approved Driving Instructor's certificate (except in Northern Ireland)

These professional instructors will give you guidance on

- What books to read
- Your practical skills
- How to study and practise
- When you are ready for your tests
- Further training after passing your practical test

It is not necessary for someone to be on the ADI Register to give training for the theory test alone. You may find a training course to help you to prepare for the test. Look in your local paper or visit your local library for information.

If you want to ride a motorcycle

Before you take your practical test you must attend and successfully complete a Compulsory Basic Training (CBT) course (except in Northern Ireland). CBT courses can only be given by training bodies approved by the DSA. Frequent checks are made to ensure a high standard of instruction.

The course will include

- Classroom training

- Practical skills training

You can find out about CBT courses from

- Your local Road Safety Officer

- Your motorcycle dealer

- The DSA
  Tel: 0115 955 7600

The DSA publication *The Motorcycling Manual* (HMSO) will tell you about motorcycling skills in more detail. Books from other publishers are also available.

You will have to answer specific questions on motorcycling in the theory test.

Ready for your test?

Make sure you are well prepared before you attempt the test. Good preparation will save you time and money.

DriveSafe Services Ltd conducts theory tests on behalf of the DSA. There are over 145 theory test centres throughout Great Britain and Northern Ireland.

Theory test sessions are available during weekdays, evenings and on Saturdays. A test appointment will be available for you within about two weeks.

You can find out where your local centre is from

- Your Approved Driving Instructor

- A DSA or DVTA driving test centre

- The telephone information line 0645 000 555

You can book your test by phoning 0645 000 666.

If you have special needs please state this on your application form. Every effort will be made to ensure the appropriate arrangements are made for you.

The test paper will be available in the following languages

English
Welsh (in Wales)
Hindi
Urdu
Gujerati
Punjabi
Bengali
Chinese

Please Note:
After January 1997 it will be necessary to pass the theory test before a booking for a practical test will be accepted. However, between 1 July 1996 and 1 January 1997 there will be a special arrangement to allow candidates to take the practical test first, if necessary. To gain a full licence in this case, the theory test must be taken within six months.

The question paper

On the first page of the paper will be practice questions. You will be given the time to look at and attempt these before the test begins.

Some of the questions in this book give 'correct answers' which don't apply to Northern Ireland.

 These are marked with NI and an explanation is given in the text.

If you are a motorcycle rider there will be specific questions on motorcycling. In this book those questions will be marked with a motorcycle symbol.

To ensure all candidates are tested fairly, questions used in the DSA theory test will be under continuous review. A few of the questions used will be changed periodically to reflect changes in legislation, or as a result of customer feedback.

If you take a DSA theory test you may find questions which don't appear in this book. The information needed to answer them is readily available in this series of *Driving Skills* (HMSO) products and *The Highway Code* (HMSO).

The question paper will have 35 questions. Attempt to answer all of them. You need to get 26 correct in order to obtain a pass.

There will be different types of questions in the paper.

MOST of them will ask you to mark ONE correct answer from four. For example:

Question
To drive on the road learners MUST

Mark one answer
- ⬭ have no penalty points on their licence
- ⬭ have taken professional instruction
- ⬭ have a signed licence
- ⬭ apply for a driving test within 12 months

Other questions will ask for TWO or more correct answers from a selection. For example:

Question
For which TWO should you use hazard warning lights?

Mark two answers
- ⬭ When you slow down quickly on a motorway because of a hazard ahead
- ⬭ When you need to park on the pavement
- ⬭ When you have broken down
- ⬭ When you wish to stop on yellow lines

Some of the questions will show you a picture. This is to test your knowledge of traffic signs or your ability to spot a hazard. Look at it carefully.

GIVE WAY
50 yds

The questions will cover a variety of topics relating to road safety. Take your time. Mark the box alongside the answers you think are correct.

Some questions will take longer to answer than others. Don't panic – you will have plenty of time.

The questions will not try to trick you. If you are well prepared you will not find the questions difficult. All 35 questions should be attempted.

You will be given 40 minutes to complete the test.

If you have learning difficulties, don't worry – you will be given extra time to complete your question paper.

When you think you have finished look at the paper again and check your answers. If you are sure about your answers hand the paper in.

The result of your test will be sent to you in fourteen days or less.

If you are taking a motorcycle theory test

As well as questions which apply to all road users you will be asked specific questions on motorcycling matters.

The topics covered in the question paper

ALERTNESS

The need to be alert and attentive when driving or riding. You must consider

- **Observation**   looking all around for other road users and pedestrians

- **Anticipation**   looking ahead and giving yourself enough time to react to hazards

- **Concentration**   being alert at all times when driving or riding

- **Awareness**   understanding the actions of other road users

- **Distraction**   not becoming distracted whilst driving or riding. Your attention must be on the road

ATTITUDE

Your attitude will affect your driving. Attitude consists of

- **Consideration**   considering other road users. Be positive but treat them as you would wish to be treated

- **Positioning**   not following too closely. As well as being dangerous, it can feel threatening to the driver in front

- **Courtesy**   treating other road users as colleagues or team members. They too are trying to complete their journey safely

- **Priority**   being aware that all rules on priority will not always be followed by other road users. Try to be calm and tolerant if other drivers or riders break the rules

SAFETY AND YOUR VEHICLE

To prevent your vehicle endangering lives you must ensure that it is in good condition. You should be aware of

- **Fault detection** being able to detect minor faults on your vehicle

- **Defects** an unroadworthy vehicle which might endanger your passengers or other road users

- **Safety equipment** if you need to use safety equipment you should know the correct way to use it

- **Emissions** your vehicle must comply with correct emissions regulations

- **Noise** vehicles are noisy. Prevent excessive noise, especially at night

SAFETY MARGINS

You must be aware of the safety margins when driving in all conditions. You should consider

- **Stopping distances** leaving enough room to stop in all conditions

- **Road surfaces** being aware of uneven or slippery surfaces

- **Skidding** preventing a skid is most important, but you should also be aware of how to react in the event of your vehicle losing control

- **Weather conditions** realising that weather conditions will have an effect on how your vehicle behaves

HAZARD AWARENESS

Your good judgement and perception of the road ahead will lessen the risk of an accident. You should keep in mind

- **Anticipation**   planning ahead to prevent last-second reactions

- **Hazard awareness**   recognising a hazard ahead and preparing yourself for it

- **Attention**   looking out for problems ahead when you are driving or riding

- **Speed and distance**   travelling at the correct speed for the situation. Leave enough distance to react if a problem arises

- **Reaction time**   being aware that you need time to react

- **Alcohol and drugs**   these will affect your reaction time

- **Tiredness**   don't drive or ride if you are tired. You need to be aware at all times

VULNERABLE ROAD USERS

Others on the road may need more time or room. Potential hazards to consider are

- **Pedestrians**   be aware of their actions as they cross the road

- **Children**   particularly unpredictable on and around roads

- **People with disabilities**   might not be able to react to danger as quickly or easily as the able-bodied

- **Motorcyclists**   be aware of their presence on the road

- **Cyclists**   may need to swerve to avoid obstructions or poor road surfaces, and are often affected by weather conditions

- **Horse riders**   animals can be unpredictable and may move rather slowly

OTHER TYPES OF VEHICLE

Other vehicles might behave differently on the road. You should consider

- **Motorcycles**   need as much room as a car
- **Lorries**   are larger and need more room on the road
- **Buses**   are usually large and might make frequent stops

VEHICLE HANDLING

You need to adapt your driving or riding to the different conditions on the road. You should be aware of

- **Weather conditions**   wet or icy roads will affect the handling of your vehicle
- **Road conditions**   the road surface may affect your vehicle
- **Time of day**   hazards when driving or riding at night
- **Speed**   it is more difficult to control your vehicle at high speeds
- **Traffic calming**   measures to slow down traffic where there are pedestrians

MOTORWAY RULES

You must know the rules which apply to you and your vehicle on the motorway. Factors to consider are

- **Speed limits**   being aware of the speed restrictions on the motorway
- **Lane discipline**   keeping to the left unless overtaking
- **Stopping**   knowing when and where you can stop on the motorway
- **Lighting**   being aware of the importance of being seen
- **Parking**   not parking on the motorway unless in an emergency

RULES OF THE ROAD

You should know the rules of the road. Aspects include

- **Speed limits** being aware of the speed limits for different types of vehicle

- **Parking** choosing a sensible place to park

- **Lighting** not letting your vehicle become a hazard

ROAD AND TRAFFIC SIGNS

Traffic signs are a means of giving messages to road users. You should know what they mean. You should consider

- **Road signs** they tell you about the road ahead

- **Speed limits** recognise signs showing speed limits

- **Road markings** directions might be painted on the road surface

- **Regulations** these can be shown to you by means of a road sign

DOCUMENTS

You and your vehicle must be licenced to be on the road. The documents you will need include

- **Licence** you must know what the law requires

- **Insurance** you must have the cover you need to drive or ride

- **MOT certificate** you must be aware of the safety checks your vehicle must undergo to gain an MOT certificate

ACCIDENTS

You should know what to do if you arrive at or are involved in an accident.
You should be aware of

- **First Aid**   if you are qualified and fit, your fast, effective action might save a life

- **Warning devices** knowing how to warn other road users of an accident

- **Reporting procedures** knowing where and when to report an accident

- **Safety regulations** knowing what to do if a vehicle carrying hazardous loads is involved in an accident

VEHICLE LOADING

You should be aware of the the importance of secure loads.
You should consider

- **Stability**   making sure that your load does not affect the stability of your vehicle

- **Towing**   being aware of the effects of towing a trailer and the rules which apply

About Part Three

In this part of the book you will find questions that might be used in the theory test. The answers have been provided to help you to study for the theory test.

DON'T JUST LEARN THE ANSWERS. It is important that you know *why* the answers are correct.

For easy reference, and to help you study, the questions have been divided into topics and put into sections. Although this is not how they are found on the question paper it will be helpful if you want to refer to particular subjects.

In this book the questions are on the left-hand side of the page. Below each question you will find the answers. Correct answers are in **bold** and are at the top of the list of options. This is for easy reference. **Please note** this is not necessarily how you will find the answers on your question paper.

On the right-hand side of the pages in this book there is a brief explanation of why the answer is correct. With this will be some advice on correct driving procedures.

Where there are similar questions on different pages the explanation will be repeated for you.

You will be given the correct answers. It is VERY important that you understand the reasons why they are correct. This will help you with your practical skills and prepare you to be a confident and safe driver.

If you find studying difficult or boring, try studying with friends. A lot of fun can be had from a question and answer game. Others in the group do not have to be studying for the test – experienced drivers might still learn something too.

If you are taking a motorcycle theory test

In Part Three the specific questions for motorcyclists are marked with a motorcycle symbol. Most of the other questions refer to all road users.

On some there will be slight changes, for example: 'rider' instead of 'driver' or 'headlight' instead of 'headlights'. You can expect to see some of these on your question paper.

This section looks at alertness and
attention when you are driving.

The questions will ask you about

- Observation
- Anticipation
- Concentration
- Awareness
- Distraction
- Boredom

Question
When turning your car in the road you should

Mark one answer ✓

- ● **check all around for other road users**
- ○ use a driveway if possible
- ○ overhang the kerb
- ○ keep your hand on the handbrake throughout

There might be an occasion when you need to turn your car around to face the opposite way. Ensure that you are fully aware of other road users by practising good observation. The road you intend to turn around in should not be busy. If it is, find a quiet side road to turn in.

Question
You are reversing into a side road. Whilst reversing you should look mainly

Mark one answer

- ● **through the rear window**
- ○ into the interior mirror
- ○ into the door mirror nearest the kerb
- ○ into the door mirror away from the kerb

When you are turning around or reversing into a side road check for other road users and pedestrians. Use your mirrors but look mainly through the rear and side windows, especially the rear window when reversing.

Question
To move off safely from a parked position you should

Mark one answer

- ● **use your mirrors and look round for a final check**
- ○ signal if other drivers will need to slow down
- ○ NOT look round if there is a parked vehicle close in front of you
- ○ give a hand signal as well as using your indicators

When moving off from the side of the road you should always use your mirrors. Look all around for a final check. There may be a road user you have not seen in your mirrors.

Question
To move off safely from a parked position you should

Mark one answer

- ● **look over your shoulder for a final check**
- ○ signal if other drivers will need to slow down
- ○ NOT look round if there is a parked vehicle close in front of you
- ○ give a hand signal as well as using your indicators

If you are intending to move off from the side of the road on a motorcycle you must take a final look around over your shoulder. There may be another road user not visible in your mirrors.

Question
What should you do just before you move off?

Mark one answer

● **Look over your right shoulder**
○ Let the clutch out quickly
○ Turn the indicators off
○ Give a continuous arm signal

Before moving off from the side of the road practise good all-round observation. Look ahead and in your mirrors, then just before you move off look over your shoulder.

Question
You want to move off from a parked position. The road is busy with traffic passing from behind. You should

Mark one answer

● **wait without signalling for a safe gap in the traffic**
○ give a signal and move away as soon as someone flashes you
○ signal while waiting for a gap in the traffic
○ edge your way into the traffic until someone gives way

If you want to move away from the side of the road and the road is busy, wait without signalling for a safe gap in the traffic. Don't immediately signal without considering what is behind you. If someone flashes their headlights, BE CAUTIOUS. Their signal may not mean what you think.

Question
Flat mirrors fitted on the handlebars make it

Mark one answer

● **easier to judge speed and distance of traffic behind**
○ less likely that your view will be spoiled by vibration
○ harder to judge speed and distance of traffic behind
○ easier to get a wide view of traffic behind

You should always be aware of what is behind you. Mirrors can either be flat or convex. Flat mirrors don't distort the picture of the road behind. This makes it easier to judge the speed and distance of following traffic. Convex mirrors are slightly curved, to give a wider field of vision. This makes it more difficult to judge the speed and direction of following traffic. However, don't rely on mirrors alone when manoeuvring.

Question
You are just about to turn right.
What should you do just before you turn?

Mark one answer

● **Take a 'lifesaver' glance over your shoulder**
○ Give the correct signal
○ Select the correct gear
○ Get in position ready for the turn

Question
What is the safest way to brake?

Mark one answer

● **Brake lightly, then harder as you begin to stop, then ease off just before stopping**
○ Brake hard, put your gear lever into neutral and pull your handbrake on just before stopping
○ Brake lightly, push your clutch pedal down and pull your handbrake on just before stopping
○ Put your gear lever into neutral, brake hard, then ease off just before stopping

Question
You see road signs showing a sharp bend ahead. What should you do?

Mark one answer

● **Slow down before the bend**
○ Continue at the same speed
○ Slow down as you go around the bend
○ Slow down as you come out of the bend

Question
In which situation should you expect other vehicles to overtake you on either side?

Mark one answer

● **In a one-way street**
○ On a dual carriageway
○ On a motorway
○ In a contraflow system

When you are turning right plan your approach to the junction. Signal and select the correct gear in good time. Just before you turn give a 'lifesaver' glance to the rear for a final check behind and alongside.

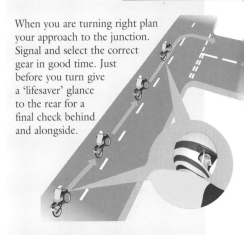

Try to plan ahead so you do not need to brake harshly. Brake lightly, then harder as you begin to stop, then ease off just before stopping. Do not put your gear lever into neutral until you come to a complete stop, as this might cause a loss of control.

Road signs might give you warning of a hazard ahead. Always look and plan well ahead. This will avoid the need for late, harsh braking. Your motorcycle should be upright and moving in a straight line when you brake. This will ensure maximum control when dealing with the hazard.

Be aware of others around you. Try to anticipate their intentions. If you are in a one-way street expect other road users to overtake on either side.

Question
You wish to overtake a long, slow-moving vehicle on a busy road.
You should

Mark one answer
- ● **keep well back until you can see it is clear**
- ○ wait behind until the driver waves you past
- ○ flash your headlights for the oncoming traffic to give way
- ○ follow it closely and keep moving out to see the road ahead

If you are following another vehicle which is travelling very slowly try to be patient. Stay well back from it so your view of the road ahead is not restricted. Wait until there is a safe place to overtake before you do so.

Question
You should ONLY use a hand-held telephone

Mark one answer
- ● **when you have stopped at a safe place**
- ○ if your vehicle has an automatic gear change
- ○ if you need to make an emergency call
- ○ when you are travelling on a minor road

A mobile telephone is a useful means of communication whilst away from home or the office. It can also be invaluable for use in an emergency or when you have broken down.

If you have a hand-held telephone always stop in a safe place before using it.

Don't use it while moving.

Question
You are driving a vehicle fitted with a hand telephone.
To answer the telephone you MUST

Mark one answer
- ● **find a safe place to stop**
- ○ reduce your speed
- ○ steer the car with one hand
- ○ be particularly careful at junctions

Your attention should be on your driving at all times. If you use your telephone frequently, especially on motorways, have your vehicle fitted with a 'hands free' telephone. In each case do not let any conversation on the phone affect your concentration.

DSA THEORY TEST for cars and motorcycles

Question
You are driving at night and are dazzled by the headlights of an oncoming car.
You should

Mark one answer

● **slow down or stop**
○ close your eyes
○ flash your headlights
○ pull down the sun visor

Question
You are riding at night and are dazzled by the headlights of an oncoming car.
You should

Mark one answer

● **slow down or stop**
○ close your eyes
○ flash your headlight
○ pull down your helmet's visor

If you are driving at night there will be extra hazards. Speeds and distances can be more difficult to judge. If the darkness makes you feel drowsy then take a rest. The lights of oncoming vehicles can often distract. If you are dazzled by them, don't

• close your eyes
• flash your headlights. This will only distract the oncoming driver too

If you are riding a motorcycle, taking a hand off the handlebars to adjust your visor might lead to loss of control. A dirty or scratched visor could cause dazzle and impair vision further.

Whether riding or driving, slow down or stop until your eyes have adjusted.

This section looks at your attitude to other road users.

The questions will ask you about

- Consideration
- Close following
- Courtesy
- Priority

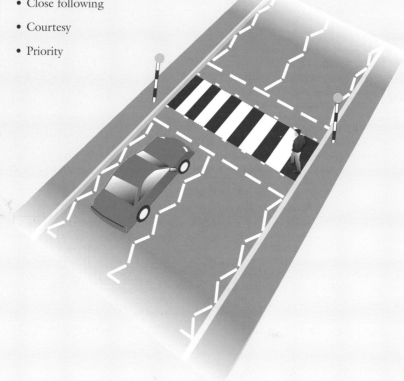

Question
At a pelican crossing the flashing amber light means you should

Mark one answer
- ● **give way to pedestrians already on the crossing**
- ○ stop, if you can do so safely
- ○ stop and wait for the green light
- ○ give way to pedestrians waiting to cross

Question
You are approaching a pelican crossing. The amber light is flashing. You must

Mark one answer
- ● **give way to pedestrians who are crossing**
- ○ encourage pedestrians to cross
- ○ not move until the green light appears
- ○ stop even if the crossing is clear

Question
You are driving towards a zebra crossing. Pedestrians are waiting to cross. You should

Mark one answer
- ● **slow down and prepare to stop**
- ○ give way to the elderly and infirm only
- ○ use your headlamps to indicate they can cross
- ○ wave at them to cross the road

Question
You are riding towards a zebra crossing. Pedestrians are waiting to cross. You should

Mark one answer
- ● **slow down and prepare to stop**
- ○ give way to the elderly and infirm only
- ○ use your headlamp to indicate they can cross
- ○ wave at them to cross the road

Pelican crossings are light-controlled crossings where pedestrians use push-button controls to change the signals. Pelican crossings have no red and amber lights before green. Instead, they have a flashing amber light which means you must give way to pedestrians on the crossing.

If it is clear you may go on.

While the pedestrians are crossing, don't

- encourage people to cross by waving or flashing your headlights – others may misunderstand your signal
- rev your engine impatiently

Zebra crossings have

- flashing amber beacons on both sides of the road
- black and white stripes on the crossing
- white zigzag markings on both sides of the crossing

Where pedestrians are waiting to cross, slow down and prepare to stop.

It is courteous to stop if you can do so safely, especially if

- anyone is waiting on the pavement with a pram or pushchair
- children or the elderly are hesitating to cross because of heavy traffic

Question

You stop for pedestrians waiting to cross at a zebra crossing.
They do not start to cross.
What should you do?

Mark one answer

● **Be patient and wait**
○ Sound your horn
○ Drive on
○ Wave them to cross

Question

You are travelling behind another vehicle at 55 mph.
What distance would you stay behind for safety?

Mark one answer

● **55 metres (180 feet)**
○ 25 metres (80 feet)
○ 45 metres (150 feet)
○ 35 metres (115 feet)

Question

A two-second gap between yourself and the car in front is sufficient when conditions are

Mark one answer

● **good**
○ wet
○ damp
○ foggy

Question

Which TWO of the following are causes of rear-end collisions?

Mark two answers

● **Not paying enough attention to the road**
● **Driving too close to the vehicle in front**
○ Traffic lights changing suddenly
○ Pedestrian crossings in busy, built-up areas
○ Stopping at every junction

If you stop for pedestrians and they do not start to cross, don't

- wave them across
- sound your horn

This could be dangerous if another vehicle is approaching and hasn't seen or heard your signal.

Be patient and wait.

Accidents are often caused by following the car in front too closely. This reduces your view of the road ahead and leaves you less time to react if you have to brake.

A good attitude will help to make you a safer driver. Always keep a safety margin.

A reasonable rule to apply is 1 metre (3 feet) for every mile an hour you are travelling.

In good, dry conditions an alert driver who is driving a vehicle with tyres and brakes in good condition needs at least two seconds from the car in front.

To measure this choose a reference point such as a bridge, sign or tree. When the vehicle ahead passes the object say to yourself 'Only a fool breaks the two-second rule.'

If you reach the object before you finish saying this you are TOO CLOSE.

Question
You are travelling on a fast road in good conditions. How can you be sure you are following at a safe distance?

Mark one answer

● **There should be a two-second time gap between you and the car in front**

○ The distance between you and the car in front should be twice the length of your vehicle

○ The distance between you and the car in front should be your braking distance

○ There should be a one-second time gap between you and the car in front

Question
You are following a vehicle on a wet road. You should leave a time gap of at least

Mark one answer

● **four seconds**

○ one second

○ two seconds

○ three seconds

Question
You are driving at the legal speed limit. A vehicle comes up quickly behind, flashing its headlamps. You should

Mark one answer

● **allow the vehicle to overtake**

○ accelerate to maintain a gap behind you

○ touch the brakes to show your brake lights

○ maintain your speed and prevent the vehicle from overtaking

Wet roads will increase the time it will take you to stop. The 'Two-Second Rule' will double to AT LEAST FOUR SECONDS.

If you are driving at the legal speed limit and the driver behind becomes impatient to overtake, let them do so. If they break the law it is their risk. Don't

- brake sharply – the driver behind might be too close
- signal them to overtake – this could lead them into another hazard
- block their progress – this will only lead to the other driver becoming more frustrated

Slow down, if necessary, pull in and let the overtaking vehicle pass.

Question

You are driving at the legal speed limit.
A vehicle behind wants to overtake.
Should you try to prevent the driver overtaking?

Mark one answer

- ● **No, not at any time**
- ○ No, unless it is safe to do so
- ○ Yes, because the other driver is acting dangerously
- ○ Yes, because the other driver is breaking the law

Don't enforce the speed limit by blocking their progress. If they wish to overtake and it means they break the law, it is their risk.

Question

You are driving in traffic at the speed limit for the road.
The driver behind is trying to overtake.
You should

Mark one answer

- ● **keep a steady course and allow the driver behind to overtake**
- ○ move closer to the car ahead, so the driver behind has no room to overtake
- ○ wave the driver behind to overtake when it is safe
- ○ accelerate to get away from the driver behind

Keep a steady course to give the driver behind an opportunity to overtake safely. Reacting to another's impatience will only lead to danger.

Question

You are driving a slow-moving vehicle on a narrow road.
When traffic wishes to overtake you should

Mark one answer

- ● **pull in safely as soon as you can**
- ○ take no action
- ○ put your hazard warning lights on
- ○ stop immediately and wave them on

Try not to hold up a queue of traffic. This might lead to other road users becoming impatient. If you are driving a slow-moving vehicle and the road is narrow pull in as soon as it is safe to do so.

Question
You are driving a slow-moving vehicle.
There is a queue of traffic behind.
You should

Mark one answer
- ● **pull in when it is safe to do so**
- ○ take no action
- ○ keep as far to the left as possible
- ○ wave the traffic past when the road is clear

Question
You are driving a slow-moving vehicle on a narrow winding road.
You should

Mark one answer
- ● **pull in safely when you can to let following vehicles overtake**
- ○ keep well out to stop vehicles overtaking dangerously
- ○ wave following vehicles past you if you think they can overtake quickly
- ○ give a left signal when it is safe for vehicles to overtake you

Question
A flashing amber light on a vehicle means

Mark one answer
- ● **a slow-moving vehicle**
- ○ an emergency vehicle travelling fast
- ○ a doctor going to an emergency
- ○ a security van carrying cash

Question
What type of emergency vehicle is fitted with a green flashing light?

Mark one answer
- ● **Doctor's car**
- ○ Fire engine
- ○ Road gritter
- ○ Ambulance

While moving keep a steady course. Don't

- put your hazard warning lights on – other traffic might think your vehicle is stationary
- stop alongside or near a hazard – the following traffic will need to overtake safely
- wave the other traffic on – other traffic may not have seen your signal
- show discourtesy by not pulling in at a safe place

Try to be courteous and considerate to other road users. Imagine how you would feel if you were the following driver or rider.

If you are following a vehicle showing a flashing amber light be cautious as it may be travelling very slowly. Or it may be attending a breakdown.

Try not to become impatient. Wait until there is a safe place to overtake or pass the vehicle.

A green flashing light on a vehicle means the driver or passenger is a doctor on an emergency call. Give way to them if it is safe to do so. Be aware that the vehicle may be travelling quickly or may stop in a hurry.

Question

A vehicle has a flashing green light. What does this mean?

Mark one answer

● **A doctor is answering an emergency call**

○ The vehicle is slow moving

○ It is a motorway police patrol vehicle

○ A vehicle is carrying hazardous chemicals

A doctor attending an emergency might show a green flashing light on his or her vehicle. Give way to them as they will need to reach their destination quickly. Be aware that they might pull over suddenly.

Question

You must take extra care when driving near trams because

Mark one answer

● **of their speed and silent approach**

○ they may stop suddenly to recharge the batteries

○ they are automatic and have no driver

○ you must NOT drive over the rails

Take care in towns where there are trams. You may not be used to dealing with the different priorities.

Modern trams travel very quickly and you may not be able to hear them approaching. The tram is not able to steer around you, it is not able to change its course.

Question

A bus is stopped at a bus stop ahead of you. Its right-hand indicator is flashing. You should

Mark one answer

● **slow down and give way if it is safe to do so**

○ flash your headlights and slow down

○ sound your horn and keep going

○ slow down and then sound your horn

Give way to buses whenever you can do so safely, especially when they signal to pull away from bus stops. Look out for people leaving the bus and crossing the road. Don't

• flash your headlights
• sound your horn
• give any other misleading signal

Question

You should ONLY flash your headlamps to other road users

Mark one answer

● **to let them know you are there**

○ to show you are giving way

○ to show you are about to reverse

○ to tell them you have right of way

You should only flash your headlamps to warn others of your presence. Don't use them to

• greet others
• show impatience
• give up your priority

Question
What should you use your horn for?

Mark one answer
● **To alert others to your presence**
○ To allow you right of way
○ To greet other road users
○ To signal your annoyance

Question
A vehicle pulls out in front of you at a junction. What should you do?

Mark one answer
● **Slow down and be ready to stop**
○ Swerve past it and blow your horn
○ Flash your headlights and drive up close behind
○ Accelerate past it immediately

Question
You are in a one-way street and want to turn right.
You should position yourself

Mark one answer
● **in the right-hand lane**
○ in the left-hand lane
○ in either lane, depending on the traffic
○ just left of the centre line

Question
You wish to turn right ahead.
Why should you take up the correct position in good time?

Mark one answer
● **To help other road users know what you intend to do**
○ To allow other drivers to pull out in front of you
○ To give a better view into the road you are joining
○ To allow drivers to pass you on the right

Only use your horn to warn other road users of your presence. Don't use it to

• greet others
• show impatience
• give priority

Your horn should not be used between 11.30 pm and 7 am in a built-up area or when your vehicle is stationary – unless a moving vehicle poses a danger.

Try to be ready for the unexpected. Plan ahead and learn to anticipate hazards. You will then give yourself more time to react to any problems which might occur.

Be tolerant of the behaviour of other road users who do not behave correctly.

If you are travelling in a one-way street and wish to turn right you should take up a position in the right-hand lane. This will enable other road users not wishing to turn to proceed on the left.

If you wish to turn right into a side road take up your position in good time. Move to the centre of the road when it is safe to do so. This will allow vehicles to pass you on the left. Early planning will show other traffic what you intend to do.

This section looks at safety and your vehicle.

The questions will ask you about

- Fault detection
- Defects and their effect on safety
- Use of safety equipment
- Emissions
- Noise

Question
Which of these, if allowed to get low, could cause an accident?

Mark one answer
- ● Brake fluid level
- ○ Anti-freeze level
- ○ Battery water level
- ○ Radiator coolant level

Question
Which FOUR of these **must** be in good working order for your car to be roadworthy?

Mark four answers
- ● Speedometer
- ● Windscreen washers
- ● Windscreen wipers
- ● Horn
- ○ Temperature gauge
- ○ Oil warning light

Question
Which FOUR of these must be in good working order for your machine to be roadworthy?

Mark four answers
- ● Speedometer
- ● Brakes
- ● Direction indicators, if fitted
- ● Horn
- ○ Tool kit
- ○ Side stand

In order to keep your vehicle in good working order you should carry out frequent checks. As a driver or rider you must ensure that you are using a safe vehicle or machine which will not endanger other road users.

If you drive a vehicle get in to the habit of checking the

- horn
- windscreen wipers
- windscreen washers
- brake fluid
- lights – get someone to help you check the brake lights
- indicators
- battery – this may be maintenance-free and not need topping up
- steering – check for 'play' in the steering wheel
- oil
- water
- suspension

Take pride in the condition of your vehicle. Keeping it in good condition will prolong its life. It will also help to keep running costs down.

If you ride a motorcycle check the

- drive chain – for tension
- horn
- brakes and brake fluid
- lights – get someone to help you check the brake lights
- indicators
- battery – this may be maintenance-free and not need topping up
- steering – check for 'play' in the steering
- oil
- water
- suspension

Whether driving or riding, check the speedometer is working once you have moved off.

Question
Which TWO are badly affected if the tyres are under-inflated?

Mark two answers
- ● **Braking**
- ● **Steering**
- ○ Changing gear
- ○ Reversing

Question
Which TWO are badly affected if the tyres are under inflated?

Mark two answers
- ● **Braking**
- ● **Steering**
- ○ Changing gear
- ○ Parking

Question
It is essential that tyre pressures are checked regularly.
When should this be done?

Mark one answer
- ● **When tyres are cold**
- ○ After any lengthy journey
- ○ After driving at high speed
- ○ When tyres are hot

Question
How often should motorcycle tyre pressures be checked?

Mark one answer
- ● **At least weekly**
- ○ Only during each regular service
- ○ After each long journey
- ○ At least monthly

The tyres on your vehicle or machine should be checked at least once a week. Incorrect tyre pressures might affect steering and braking.

Low pressure produces a heavier feel and might cause the tyres to overheat. It can also affect both road holding and tyre wear, due to the side walls flexing.

Your tyres are your only grip on the road and therefore very important to your safety.

If you are not sure of the correct tyre pressures check the vehicle handbook. If you do not have one, go to a garage where a chart showing the correct pressures is displayed.

Incorrect tyre pressures will affect steering and braking so it is very important that you take the time to attend to them. Correct tyre pressures can reduce the risk of skidding and will provide a more comfortable ride.

When you check the tyre pressures do so when the tyres are cold. This will give you a more accurate reading. The heat generated from a long journey will raise the pressure inside the tyre.

As a motorcyclist your tyres are vital to your safety. Make sure you check the pressure in your tyres at least once a week. Don't ride your machine if the tyres are incorrectly inflated.

Question
What is the most important factor in avoiding running into the car in front?

Mark one answer

● **Keeping the correct separation distance**
○ Making sure your brakes are efficient
○ Always driving at a steady speed
○ Having tyres that meet the legal requirements

Question
The legal minimum depth of tread for car tyres is

Mark one answer

● **1.6 mm**
○ 2.5 mm
○ 4 mm
○ 1 mm

Question
The legal minimum depth of tread for motorcycle tyres is

Mark one answer

● **1 mm**
○ 2.5 mm
○ 4 mm
○ 1.6 mm

Question
You are riding a machine of more than 50cc. Which FOUR would make a tyre illegal?

Mark four answers

● **Tread less than 1 mm deep**
● **A large bulge in the wall**
● **A recut tread**
● **Exposed ply or cord**
○ Tread less than 1.6 mm deep
○ A stone wedged in the tread

Having tyres in a good condition and at the correct pressure will not take away all the risks when driving or riding. Leaving a correct separation distance and planning well ahead will help to make you a safer driver.

Tyres must have a good depth of tread. The legal limit for cars is a minimum of 1.6 mm. This depth should be throughout the central three-quarters of the breadth of the tyre and around the entire circumference.

The legal limit of tyre tread for motorcycles (over 50cc) is a minimum of 1 mm. The entire original tread should be continuous. Don't ride a machine with worn tyres.

Your tyres are your only contact with the road so it is very important that you ensure they are in good condition. When checking them make sure there are no bulges or cuts in the side walls. Always buy your tyres from a reputable dealer to ensure quality and value for money.

Question

Excessive or uneven tyre wear can be caused by faults in which THREE ?

Mark three answers

● **The braking system**
● **Wheel alignment**
● **The suspension**
○ The gearbox
○ The accelerator
○ The exhaust system

Uneven wear on your tyres can be caused by the condition of your vehicle. Have it serviced regularly so that the brakes, steering and wheel alignment are checked.

Question

What does this warning light on the instrument panel mean?

Mark one answer

● **Hazard flashers**
○ Warning triangle
○ Main beam
○ Handbrake on

Get to know the vehicle you are driving. Before moving off ensure that you understand the function of any switches, gauges and controls. If you are not sure about any of them read the handbook. This will give you information about the instrument panel and show you where warning lights are situated.

Question

Your vehicle pulls to one side when you brake. What is the most likely fault?

Mark one answer

● **Poorly adjusted brakes**
○ Low brake fluid level
○ Your handbrake is still on
○ Incorrect tyre pressures

If you find that your vehicle is pulling to one side when you brake have your vehicle checked by a qualified mechanic. It could mean that the brakes are faulty or incorrectly adjusted.

DSA THEORY TEST for cars and motorcycles

Question
Your vehicle pulls to one side when braking.
You should

Mark one answer

● consult your garage as soon as
possible ✓

○ change the tyres around

○ pump the pedal when braking

○ use your handbrake at the same time

The brakes on your vehicle or machine
must be effective and properly adjusted.
If your vehicle pulls to one side when
braking take it to be checked by a
qualified mechanic.

Question
If you notice a strong smell of petrol as you drive
along you should ✓

Mark one answer

● stop and investigate the problem

○ not worry, as it is only exhaust fumes

○ carry on at a reduced speed

○ expect it to stop in a few miles

If there is a strong smell of petrol or
fuel as you drive STOP and investigate.
Don't smoke or put naked lights
anywhere near the leakage. Have it
checked by a qualified mechanic as soon
as possible.

Question
When are you allowed to drive if your brake lights
do NOT work?

Mark one answer

● At no time

○ During the daytime

○ When going for an MOT test

○ In an emergency

Before you drive or ride you must ensure
that all your lights are in good working
order. All lights on your vehicle must be
capable of working whether it is day or
night. Get someone to help you check
the brake lights. Don't drive if they are
not working.

Question
When may you use hazard warning lights?

Mark one answer

● When you have broken down

○ To park alongside another car

○ To park on double yellow lines

○ When you are being towed

Hazard warning lights may be used to
warn other road users when you

- have broken down and are
  causing an obstruction
- are on a motorway and want
  to warn the traffic behind you of
  a hazard ahead

DON'T use them

- when being towed
- when stopped in a restricted area,
  unless you are causing a hazard

Question
Hazard warning lights should be used when vehicles are

Mark one answer

⬤ **broken down and causing an obstruction**
◯ faulty and moving slowly
◯ being towed along a road
◯ reversing into a side road

Question
It is important to wear suitable shoes when you are driving.
Why is this?

Mark one answer

⬤ **To maintain safe control of the pedals**
◯ To prevent wear on the pedal rubbers
◯ To enable you to make quicker gear changes
◯ To enable you to walk for assistance if you break down

Question
What will reduce the risk of neck injury resulting from a collision?

Mark one answer

⬤ **A properly adjusted head restraint**
◯ An air-sprung seat
◯ Anti-lock brakes
◯ A collapsible steering wheel

Question
You should NOT ride in trainers and shorts because

Mark one answer

⬤ **there is not enough protection for your feet or legs in an accident**
◯ there will not be enough grip on the footrests
◯ the weather may change while you are out
◯ you will not be able to operate the stand properly

There must be a warning light on the control panel to show when the hazard lights are in operation. Don't forget to switch them off when you move away.

When you are driving or riding ensure that you are wearing comfortable clothing. Comfortable shoes will ensure that you have proper control over the foot pedals.

Head restraints will reduce the risk of neck injury if you are involved in a collision. They must be properly adjusted. Make sure they aren't positioned too low, as in an accident they could cause damage to the neck.

Driving with good forward planning and anticipation will prevent you having to brake harshly, though there might be the occasion when you have to stop suddenly in an emergency.

When riding a motorcycle it is essential that you wear the appropriate clothing. Training shoes will not give you the protection you need. Strong boots will protect your feet, ankles and calves from knocks on the footrest or kick-start lever. They will also reduce the risk of injury if you have an accident.

Question
You are riding a motorcycle in very hot weather. You should

Mark one answer
- ● **continue to wear protective clothing**
- ○ ride with your visor fully open
- ○ wear trainers instead of boots
- ○ slacken your helmet strap

Question
Why should you wear fluorescent clothing when riding in daylight?

Mark one answer
- ● **It helps other road users to see you**
- ○ It reduces wind resistance
- ○ It prevents injury if you come off the machine
- ○ It keeps you cool in hot weather

Question
Why should riders wear reflective clothing?

Mark one answer
- ● **To be seen better at night**
- ○ To protect them from the cold
- ○ To protect them from direct sunlight
- ○ To be seen better in daylight

In very hot weather it is tempting to ride in light summer clothes. Don't do this. If you fall from your machine you will have no protection from the hard road surface. Always wear your protective clothing, whatever the weather.

When riding a motorcycle it is very important that other road users are able to see you clearly. Fluorescent clothing will help towards this, reducing the risk of an accident. You must be visible from all sides.

Reflective strips

Reflective patches

Reflective clothing shows up in the dark and

- reflects the lights of other vehicles
- makes sure you are visible from long distances

Question

You are carrying two children and their parents in your car.
Who is responsible for seeing that the children wear seat belts?

Mark one answer

● **You**
○ The children's parents
○ The front-seat passenger
○ The children

Seat belts save lives and reduce the risk of injury. You MUST wear a seat belt unless you are exempt. There are also legal requirements for your passengers. Make sure you know the rules for wearing seat belts. Check the chart below.

	FRONT SEAT	REAR SEAT	RESPONSIBILITY
Driver	Seat belt must be worn if fitted		Driver
Child under three years	Appropriate child restraint must be worn	Appropriate child restraint must be worn if available	Driver
Child aged three to eleven and under 1.5 metres (about 5 feet)	Appropriate child restraint must be worn if available. If not, an adult seat belt must be worn	Appropriate child restriant must be worn if available. If not, an adult seat belt must be worn if available.	Driver
Child aged 12 or 13 or a younger child 1.5 metres in height (about 5 feet) or more	Adult seat belt must be worn if available	Adult seat belt must be worn if available	Driver
Adult passengers	Seat belt must be worn if available	Seat belt must be worn if available	Passenger

Question

Car passengers MUST wear a seat belt if one is available, unless they are

Mark one answer

● **exempt for medical reasons**
○ under 14 years old
○ under 1.5 metres (5 feet) in height
○ sitting in the-rear seat

DSA THEORY TEST for cars and motorcycles

Question

A car driver MUST ensure that seat belts are worn by

Mark one answer

⬤ **children under 14**
⭕ all front-seat passengers
⭕ all passengers
⭕ all rear-seat passengers

Study the chart regarding seat belts. You could be responsible for your passenger wearing the appropriate restraints.

Question

Your safety helmet has a small crack. You should

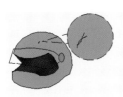

Mark one answer

⬤ **get a new one before riding**
⭕ ride at low speeds only
⭕ ask the police to inspect it
⭕ have it repaired by an expert

If you damage your motorcycle helmet, even slightly, buy a new one. The smallest damage can make a helmet unreliable. A little expense now may save your life later.

Question

Your visor becomes badly scratched. You should

Mark one answer

⬤ **replace it**
⭕ polish with a fine abrasive
⭕ wash it in soapy water
⭕ clean it with petrol

Your visor protects your eyes from wind, rain, insects and road dirt. It is therefore important to keep it clean and in good repair. A badly scratched visor might

• obscure your view
• cause dazzle from lights of oncoming vehicles

Question
In which of these containers may you carry petrol in a motor vehicle?

A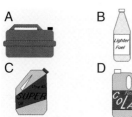

B

C

D

Mark one answer
- ● A
- ○ B
- ○ C
- ○ D

Petrol may be carried in your vehicle but it must be carried in a container designed for that purpose. Don't use other types as these might leak or perish. Suitable containers are available in most motor shops and petrol stations.

Question
You must NOT sound your horn

Mark one answer
- ● **between 11.30 pm and 7 am in a built-up area**
- ○ between 10 pm and 6 am in a built-up area
- ○ at any time in a built-up area
- ○ between 11.30 pm and 6 am on any road

Vehicles can be noisy. Every effort must be made to prevent excessive noise, especially in built-up areas at night. Don't

- rev the engine
- sound the horn between 11.30 pm and 7 am (unless it is necessary to warn a moving vehicle)

Question
When should you NOT use your horn in a built-up area?

Mark one answer
- ● **Between 11.30 pm and 7 am**
- ○ Between 8 pm and 8 am
- ○ Between 9 pm and dawn
- ○ Between dusk and 8 am

Question
You cannot see clearly behind when reversing. What should you do?

Mark one answer
- ● **Ask someone to guide you**
- ○ Open your window to look behind
- ○ Open the door and look behind
- ○ Look in the nearside mirror

If you want to turn your car around try to find a place where you have good all-round vision. If this is not possible and you are unable to see clearly then get someone to guide you.

DSA THEORY TEST for cars and motorcycles

Question

When must you use a dipped headlight during the day?

Mark one answer

- ● **In poor visibility**
- ○ On country roads
- ○ Along narrow streets
- ○ When parking

It will help other road users to see you if you use dipped headlights during the day. If there is limited visibility you MUST use them.

Question

Your side stand is not fully up when you start to ride.
What could this do?

Mark one answer

- ● **Dig into the ground when you are cornering**
- ○ Alter the machine's centre of gravity
- ○ Catch on your feet
- ○ Cause the machine to steer badly

Make sure your side stand is fully up before you move off. If it is not up it could dig into the ground as you move away and might lead to an accident.

Question

What should you NEVER do at a petrol station?

Mark one answer

- ● **Smoke**
- ○ Run about
- ○ Eat
- ○ Wash

Petrol stations are good places to stop and check your vehicle or machine. Use the facilities on offer to refuel or clean your vehicle or machine. Relax but NEVER smoke on the forecourt. This is hazardous and a major fire risk.

This section looks at safety margins and how they can be affected by conditions.

The questions will ask you about

- Stopping distances
- Road surfaces
- Skidding
- Weather conditions

Question
Stopping in good conditions at 30 mph takes at least

Mark one answer
- ● **six car lengths**
- ○ two car lengths
- ○ three car lengths
- ○ one car length

Question
You are on a good, dry road surface and in a vehicle with good brakes and tyres.
What is the shortest overall stopping distance at 40 mph?

Mark one answer
- ● **36 metres (120 feet)**
- ○ 23 metres (75 feet)
- ○ 96 metres (315 feet)
- ○ 53 metres (175 feet)

Question
What is the braking distance at 50 mph?

Mark one answer
- ● **38 metres (125 feet)**
- ○ 55 metres (180 feet)
- ○ 24 metres (79 feet)
- ○ 14 metres (45 feet)

Question
You are driving in good conditions at 55 mph. What is a safe minimum distance between you and the vehicle in front?

Mark one answer
- ● **55 metres (180 feet)**
- ○ 35 metres (117 feet)
- ○ 65 metres (215 feet)
- ○ 75 metres(245 feet)

It is very important that you know your overall stopping distance at all speeds. Stopping distances increase dramatically as road speed increases. Knowing your stopping distance will reduce the risk of an accident as you will know how much room you need to leave between you and the vehicle in front.

Factors which affect how long it takes you to stop include

- how fast you are going
- whether you are travelling on the level, uphill or downhill
- the weather and road conditions
- the condition of tyres, brakes and suspension
- your reaction times

Stopping distance can be divided into

- thinking distance
- braking distance

The thinking distance is how far you travel from the moment you see the **need** to brake to the moment you **apply** the brakes.

The braking distance is how far you travel from the moment you first apply the brakes to the point where you stop.

Question
What is the shortest stopping distance at
70 mph?

Mark one answer

⬤ **96 metres (315 feet)**
◯ 53 metres (175 feet)
◯ 60 metres (200 feet)
◯ 73 metres (240 feet)

At 30 mph

Thinking   Braking   Overall stopping
distance   distance   distance
9m (30ft) 14m (45ft) 23m (75ft)

At 50 mph

Thinking   Braking   Overall stopping
distance   distance   distance
15m (50ft)   38m (125ft)   53m (175ft)

At 70 mph

Thinking   Braking   Overall stopping
distance   distance   distance
21m (70ft)   75m (245ft)   96m (315ft)

Question
You are driving at 50 mph in good conditions.
What would be your shortest stopping distance?

Mark one answer

⬤ **53 metres (175 feet)**
◯ 23 metres (75 feet)
◯ 36 metres (120 feet)
◯ 73 metres (240 feet)

Stopping distances can be difficult to
visualise. Try thinking in terms that
mean something to you. This could be

• car or motorcycle lengths
• the 100 metre sprint
• the length of a football pitch
  (which is about 100 metres/
  330 feet)

DSA THEORY TEST for cars and motorcycles

Question
You are travelling at 50 mph on a good, dry road.
What is your overall stopping distance?

Mark one answer
- ● **53 metres (175 feet)**
- ○ 36 metres (120 feet)
- ○ 75 metres (245 feet)
- ○ 96 metres (315 feet)

Question
What is the shortest overall stopping distance
on a dry road from 60 mph?

Mark one answer
- ● **73 metres (240 feet)**
- ○ 53 metres (175 feet)
- ○ 58 metres (190 feet)
- ○ 96 metres (315 feet)

Question
You are on a fast, open road in good conditions.
For safety, the distance between you and the
vehicle in front should be

Mark one answer
- ● **a two-second time gap**
- ○ one car length
- ○ 2 metres (7 feet)
- ○ two car lengths

One useful method of checking
that you have allowed enough room
between you and the vehicle in front
is the 'Two-Second Rule'.

You should allow a two-second
time gap as a safe separation distance.
Begin by saying the phrase 'Only a
fool breaks the two-second rule'
when the vehicle in front passes a
fixed point. You should not reach that
point before you finish saying the
phrase. If you do, you are travelling
too close and should drop back.

Question
Your overall stopping distance will be much longer when driving

Mark one answer
- ● **in the rain**
- ○ in fog
- ○ at night
- ○ in strong winds

Extra care should be taken in wet weather. Wet roads will affect the time it takes you to stop. Your stopping distance could be at least doubled.

Question
On a wet road what is the safest way to stop?

Mark one answer
- ● **Use both brakes**
- ○ Change gear without braking
- ○ Use the back brake only
- ○ Use the front brake only

Motorcyclists need to take extra care when stopping on wet road surfaces. Plan well ahead so that you are able to brake in good time. You should

- ensure your machine is upright
- apply both front and rear brakes evenly
- brake when travelling in a straight line

Question
Road surface is very important to motorcyclists. Which FOUR of these are more likely to reduce the stability of your machine?

Mark four answers
- ● **Pot-holes**
- ● **Drain covers**
- ● **Oil patches**
- ● **Loose gravel**
- ○ concrete
- ○ tarmac

Apart from the weather conditions, the road surface can affect the stability of a motorcycle. Try to avoid riding

- over pot-holes
- on loose surfaces and gravel
- over drain covers (especially when wet)
- over oily surfaces

Other road surfaces to watch out for are

- wet mud and leaves
- tar banding
- road markings
- tram lines

Question
What is the main reason why your stopping distance is longer after heavy rain?

Mark one answer
- ● **Your tyres will have less grip on the road**
- ○ You may not be able to see large puddles
- ○ The brakes will be cold because they are wet
- ○ Water on the windscreen will blur your view of the road ahead

When the roads are wet the water will reduce your tyres' grip on the road. When the tyres lose their grip you lose control.

You can cause the tyres to lose their grip by

- excessive acceleration (wheelspin)
- cornering too fast
- braking too hard
- harsh steering (swerving)

Question
You are driving in heavy rain when your steering suddenly becomes very light.
To get control again you must

Mark one answer
- ● **ease off the accelerator**
- ○ change down to a lower gear
- ○ brake lightly to reduce speed
- ○ steer towards a dry part of the road

Question
You are riding in heavy rain when your rear wheel skids as you accelerate.
To get control again you must

Mark one answer
- ● **ease off the throttle**
- ○ change down to a lower gear
- ○ brake to reduce speed
- ○ put your feet down

Question
You have driven through a flood.
What is the first thing you should do?

Mark one answer
- ● **Test your brakes**
- ○ Stop and check the tyres
- ○ Stop and dry the brakes
- ○ Switch on your windscreen wipers

Question
Braking distances on ice can be

Mark one answer
- ● **ten times normal distance**
- ○ twice normal distance
- ○ five times normal distance
- ○ seven times normal distance

If you find that your steering becomes light your tyres are losing their grip on the road. To regain control ease off the accelerator. Don't

- brake
- push the clutch down
- steer sharply in any direction

Bike skidding to the left

Direction of steering to correct skid

- *Ease off brake*
- *Steer to left*

If you feel your back wheel beginning to skid as you pull away ease off the throttle. This will give your rear tyre the chance to grip the road and stop the skid.

After passing through a flood or ford test your brakes. Before you do so make sure you check behind for following traffic. Don't brake sharply. The vehicle behind may not be able to stop quickly. If necessary signal your intentions.

The stopping distance will also be affected by icy and snowy weather. You need to take extra care and expect your stopping distance to increase by up to ten times the normal distance.

Question

Freezing conditions will affect the distance it takes you to come to a stop.
You should expect stopping distances to increase by up to

Mark one answer

● **ten times**
○ two times
○ five times
○ three times

You must take the road and weather conditions into account when driving. It may take ten times the distance to stop.

Question

When driving in icy conditions, the steering becomes light because the tyres

Mark one answer

● **have less grip on the road**
○ have more grip on the road
○ are too soft
○ are too hard

In icy conditions the tyres will lose much of their grip on the road. This could result in the steering becoming light. If you ease off the accelerator you should regain some steering control.

Question

You are driving on an icy road.
How can you avoid wheelspin?

Mark one answer

● **Drive at a slow speed in as high a gear as possible**
○ Use the handbrake if the wheels start to slip
○ Brake gently and repeatedly
○ Drive in a low gear at all times

If you are travelling on an icy road you should try to avoid any loss of control. You can reduce wheelspin by driving

- at a slow speed
- in as high a gear as possible

Question

How can you avoid wheelspin when driving in freezing conditions?

Mark one answer

● **Drive in as high a gear as possible**
○ Stay in first gear all the time
○ Put on your handbrake if the wheels begin to slip
○ Allow the vehicle to coast in neutral

DSA THEORY TEST for cars and motorcycles

Question
You are driving in freezing conditions.
Which THREE should you do when approaching
a sharp bend?

Mark three answers

- ● **Slow down before you reach the bend**
- ● **Drive in as high a gear as you can**
- ● **Avoid sudden steering movements**
- ○ Accelerate into the bend
- ○ Gently apply your handbrake
- ○ Keep your clutch down throughout

Question
When riding in extremely cold conditions what
can you do to keep warm?

Mark one answer

- ● **Wear suitable clothing**
- ○ Stay close in behind the vehicles in front
- ○ Lie flat on the tank
- ○ Put your hands one at a time on the
  exhaust pipe

Question
You are turning left on a slippery road.
The back of your vehicle slides to the right.
What should you do?

Mark one answer

- ● **Steer carefully to the right**
- ○ Brake firmly and do not turn the steering
  wheel
- ○ Use the clutch and brake firmly
- ○ Turn only to the left

When you are approaching a sharp
bend and the road is likely to be icy

- slow down before you reach the
  bend
- drive in as high a gear as you
  can
- avoid sudden steering
  movements

Don't

- accelerate into the bend
- apply your handbrake
- coast (hold the clutch down)

Motorcyclists are exposed to the
elements and can become very cold
when riding in wintry conditions.
It is important to keep warm or
concentration could be affected.
The only way to stay warm is to
wear suitable clothing.

If you do find yourself getting cold
then stop at a suitable place to warm
up.

If you are turning and you feel the
back of your vehicle slide to one side
steer carefully in the same direction
that the back is sliding. This should
stop the sliding and allow you to
regain control. Don't

- use the accelerator
- use the brakes
- use the clutch

Question
You are braking on a wet road.
Your vehicle begins to skid.
What is the first thing you should do?

Mark one answer

● **Release the brake fully**
○ Quickly pull up the handbrake
○ Push harder on the brake pedal
○ Put your foot on the clutch

Question
How can you tell when you are driving over black ice?

Mark one answer

● **Your steering would feel light**
○ It would be easier to brake
○ The noise from your tyres would sound louder
○ You would see black ice on the road

If the skid has been caused by braking too hard for the conditions release the brake. This will allow the wheels to turn and so limit the skid.

Skids are much easier to get into than they are to get out of. Prevention is better than cure. Stay alert to the road and weather conditions. Never drive so fast that you can't stop within the distance you can see to be clear.

Sometimes you may not be able to see that the road is icy. Black ice makes the road look damp. The signs that you are travelling on black ice can be

• the steering feels light
• the noise from your tyres suddenly goes quiet

**Rear of car skids
to the right**

**Driver steers
to the right**

Question
Coasting the vehicle

Mark one answer

● **reduces the driver's control**
○ improves the driver's control
○ makes steering easier
○ uses more fuel

'Coasting' is the term used when the clutch is held down and the vehicle is freewheeling. This reduces the driver's control of the vehicle. When you coast the engine can't drive the wheels nor can it hold the car back.

Question
When driving in snow it is best to keep in as high a gear as possible.
Why is this?

Mark one answer
- ● **To help to prevent wheelspin**
- ○ To help you slow down quickly when you brake
- ○ So that wheelspin does not cause your engine to run too fast
- ○ To leave a lower gear available in case of wheelspin

If the ground is covered in snow move off in as high a gear as possible. Stay in the highest gear you can. This reduces the power to the wheels and so lessens the chance of skidding.

Question
When driving in fog in daylight you should use

Mark one answer
- ● **dipped headlights**
- ○ sidelights
- ○ full beam headlights
- ○ hazard lights

Do not drive in fog unless you really have to. Use dipped headlights during daylight. If the visibility is below 100 metres (330 feet) use fog lights and high intensity rear lights. Let other road users know you are there.

Question
You are at a junction with limited visibility.
You should

Mark one answer
- ● **inch forward, looking both ways**
- ○ inch forward, looking to the right
- ○ inch forward, looking to the left
- ○ be ready to move off quickly

At some road junctions you might find that you can't see clearly into the road you are joining. Before you commit yourself you have to inch foward, looking both ways. Only emerge when you can see it is safe to do so. Don't

- speed out hoping the way will be clear
- look one way only

Question
Why is it good to ride with a dipped headlight in daylight?

Mark one answer
- ● **It helps other road users to see you**
- ○ It means you can ride faster
- ○ Other vehicles tend to get out of the way
- ○ They will already be on when it gets dark

Motorcycles are much smaller than other motor vehicles. This makes them difficult to see and they are easily lost from view. Riding with your dipped headlight on during the day will help other road users to see you.

Question
In very hot weather the road surface can get soft.
Which TWO of the following will be affected most?

Mark two answers
- ⬤ **The steering**
- ⬤ **The brakes**
- ◯ The suspension
- ◯ The windscreen

During hot weather the road surface can become soft. Take care when braking or cornering. Tyres do not grip well on soft tarmac.

Question
In very hot weather the road surface can get soft.
Which TWO of the following will be affected most?

Mark two answers
- ⬤ **The grip of the tyres**
- ⬤ **The brakes**
- ◯ The suspension
- ◯ The exhaust

Question
You are riding in very hot weather.
What are TWO effects that melting tar has on the control of your machine?

Mark two answers
- ⬤ **It can make the surface slippery**
- ⬤ **It can reduce tyre grip**
- ◯ It can reduce stopping distances
- ◯ It can improve braking efficiency

In hot weather never be tempted to ride without protective clothing. If you fall from your machine you will have no protection from the hard road surface.

Question
Where are you most likely to be affected by a crosswind?

Mark one answer
- ⬤ **On an open stretch of road**
- ◯ On a narrow country lane
- ◯ On a busy stretch of road
- ◯ On a long, straight road

In windy conditions care must be taken on exposed roads. A strong gust of wind can blow you off course. Watch out for other road users who may be affected more than you, such as

- cyclists
- motorcyclists
- high-sided lorries
- vehicles towing trailers

Question
You are overtaking a lorry.
There is a strong wind from the left.
As you clear the lorry you will

Mark one answer
- ⬤ **be blown away from the lorry**
- ◯ be pulled towards the lorry
- ◯ be slowed down by the crosswind
- ◯ be speeded up by the crosswind

If you overtake a lorry and there is a strong wind blowing from the left the lorry will shield you as you ride past. As you clear the lorry you will emerge into the wind blast. This will blow you to the right, away from the lorry. Be prepared to compensate.

DSA THEORY TEST for cars and motorcycles

Question
In windy conditions you need to take extra care when

Mark one answer

- ● **passing pedal cyclists**
- ○ using the brakes
- ○ making a hill start
- ○ turning into a narrow road

When overtaking cyclists give them extra room if it is windy. A sudden gust of wind could blow them off course.

Question
Your indicators may be difficult to see in bright sunlight.
What should you do?

Mark one answer

- ● **Give an arm signal as well as using your indicator**
- ○ Put your indicator on earlier
- ○ Touch the brake several times to show the stop lamp
- ○ Turn as quickly as you can

Indicators on some smaller motorcycles are difficult to see in bright sunlight. If you feel your signal might not be seen then give an arm signal as well.

Question
What should you do to help you see at night?

Mark one answer

- ● **Keep your visor or goggles clean**
- ○ Allow a gap beneath your visor or goggles
- ○ Wear a tinted visor or goggles
- ○ Don't use a visor or goggles at all

If you are riding a motorcycle at night it is important that you can see clearly. Keep your visor or goggles clean and without smears. Don't wear a tinted visor or goggles at night.

Question
You are about to go down a steep hill.
To control the speed of your vehicle you should

Mark one answer

- ● **select a low gear and use the brakes carefully**
- ○ select a high gear and use the brakes carefully
- ○ select a high gear and use the brakes firmly
- ○ select a low gear and avoid using the brakes

When travelling down a steep hill your vehicle will tend to increase speed. This will also make it more difficult for you to stop. To maintain control and prevent the vehicle running away

- • select a lower gear – the engine will then help to control your speed
- • use the brakes carefully

Question

You are on a long, downhill slope.
What should you do to help control the speed of your vehicle?

Mark one answer

⬤ **Select a low gear**
◯ Grip the steering wheel tightly
◯ Select neutral
◯ Put the clutch down

Selecting a low gear when travelling downhill will help you to control your speed. The engine will assist the brakes and prevent your vehicle gathering speed.

Question

You wish to park facing downhill.
What THREE things should you do?

Mark three answers

⬤ **Turn the steering wheel towards the kerb**
⬤ **Put the handbrake on**
⬤ **Put the vehicle into reverse gear**
◯ Park close to the bumper of another car
◯ Park with two wheels up on the kerb

If you are going to park on a hill you need to make sure the vehicle can't roll away. To be certain it is parked safely

- put the handbrake on
- put the gear lever into reverse gear
- turn the steering wheel towards the kerb

Question

You are driving in a built-up area.
You approach a speed hump.
You should

Mark one answer

⬤ **slow your vehicle right down**
◯ move across to the left-hand side of the road
◯ wait for any pedestrians to cross
◯ stop and check both pavements

Many towns have speed humps to slow down traffic. They are often where there are pedestrians, so

- slow right down when driving over them
- if you drive too fast it might affect your steering and suspension
- look out for pedestrians

Question
When approaching a right-hand bend you should keep well to the left.
Why is this?

Mark one answer

● **It improves your view of the road**
○ To overcome the effect of the road's slope
○ It lets faster traffic from behind overtake
○ To be positioned safely if the vehicle skids

Question
You are coming up to a right-hand bend.
You should

Mark one answer

● **keep well to the left for a better view around the bend**
○ keep well to the left as it makes the bend faster
○ keep well to the right to avoid anything in the gutter
○ keep well to the right to make the bend less sharp

When you have to drive around a right-hand bend you should keep to the left. This improves your view of the road ahead. Don't

- move over to the right to try and straighten the bend. You could endanger yourself by getting too close to oncoming traffic

- cross or straddle unbroken white lines along the centre of the road

- drive so fast that you can't stop within your range of vision

SECTION 5 HAZARD AWARENESS

This section looks at judgement and hazard perception.

The questions will ask you about

- Anticipation
- Hazard awareness
- Attention
- Speed and distance
- Reaction time
- The effects of alcohol and drugs
- Tiredness

Question
What is the main hazard shown in this picture?

Mark one answer
- ● **The cyclist crossing the road**
- ○ Vehicles turning right
- ○ Vehicles doing U-turns
- ○ Parked cars around the corner

Question
Which road user has caused a hazard?

Mark one answer
- ● **The parked car (arrowed A)**
- ○ The pedestrian waiting to cross (arrowed B)
- ○ The moving car (arrowed C)
- ○ The car turning (arrowed D)

Some of the questions in this section will show you a picture. Look at the picture carefully and try to imagine you are there.

The cyclist in this picture is not crossing the road in the correct place. You must be able to deal with the unexpected, especially when you are planning your approach to a hazardous junction. There will be several things to think about on your approach, so look well ahead to give yourself time to deal with them. If you need to change lanes or direction use your mirror, signal and manoeuvre in good time.

The car has parked on the approach to a pedestrian crossing. The road is marked with white zigzag lines. Don't park on these – they are there for a reason. Parking here will

- block the view for pedestrians wishing to cross the road
- restrict the view of the crossing for traffic approaching

Question

What should the cars on the pelican crossing have done?

Mark one answer

● **Left a space in the queue of traffic**
○ Got closer to the cars in front
○ Put their hazard warning lights on
○ Waited before the zigzag lines

If you are in a line of slow-moving traffic don't stop directly on the crossing. Try to judge the flow of traffic in front and leave a gap for pedestrians to cross.

Question

What should the driver of the white car do?

Mark one answer

● **Drive on slowly**
○ Stop and let the pedestrian cross
○ Wave the pedestrian to go back
○ Stop only if there is a car behind

When driving or riding through a built-up area extra care must be taken. If there are shops expect several pedestrians.

BE AWARE.

Pedestrians may have their minds on other things or be in a hurry. They might step out into the road. Don't signal or wave at a pedestrian to cross the road. Other road users may not have seen your signal and this could lead the pedestrian into a hazardous situation.

Question

What should the driver of the car approaching the crossing do?

Mark one answer

● **Slow and get ready to stop**
○ Continue at the same speed
○ Sound the horn
○ Drive through quickly

Look well ahead to see if any hazards are developing. This will give you more time to deal with them in the correct way. The man in the picture is clearly intending to cross the road. You should be travelling at a speed which allows you to check your mirror, slow down and stop in good time. You should not have to brake harshly.

Question
What should the driver of the red car do?

Mark one answer

● Wait for the pedestrian in the road to cross

○ Wave the pedestrians who are waiting to cross

○ Quickly drive behind the pedestrian in the road

○ Tell the pedestrian in the road she should not have crossed

Question
What THREE things should the driver of the grey car be specially aware of?

Mark three answers

● Pedestrians stepping out between cars

● Cars leaving parking spaces

● Parked cars' doors opening

○ The bumpy road surface

○ Empty parking spaces

○ Other cars behind the grey car

Some people might take longer to cross the road. They may be elderly or have a disability. Be patient and don't hurry them by showing your impatience. They might have poor eyesight or not be able to hear traffic approaching.

Don't signal or wave the pedestrian to cross the road. Other road users may not have seen your signal and this could lead the pedestrian into a hazardous situation.

Your awareness in hazardous situations is very important. In a busy street like the one in the picture there are many potential dangers. You might not be able to see a pedestrian crossing from between the parked vehicles. A driver or passenger of a parked car might open a door.

Drive or ride at a speed that will allow you to stop in good time if a hazard suddenly appears. It could happen at any time.

Question

What should the driver of the red car (arrowed) do?

Mark one answer

● **Wait until the car blocking the way has moved**

○ Sound the horn to tell other drivers where he is

○ Squeeze through the gap

○ Wave the driver of the white car to go on

Question

What should the driver of the grey car (arrowed) do?

Mark one answer

● **Cross if the way is clear**

○ Reverse out of the box junction

○ Wait in the same place until the lights are green

○ Wait until the lights are red then cross

If you are moving in slow-moving traffic think ahead so you don't block junctions or stop other's progress. Don't

- force others to give way to you
- sound the horn to gain priority
- flash your lights to gain or give priority
- give any other misleading signal

Yellow markings are marked on the road to prevent busy junctions becoming blocked with traffic. Don't enter the box unless your exit road is clear.

When turning right you can wait in the box if your exit road is clear but you can't proceed due to the oncoming traffic.

DSA THEORY TEST for cars and motorcycles

Question
What should the driver of a car coming up to this level crossing do?

Mark one answer
- ⬤ **Stop before the barrier**
- ◯ Drive through quickly
- ◯ Drive through carefully
- ◯ Switch on hazard warning lights

Question
What are TWO main hazards a driver should be aware of when driving along this street?

Mark two answers
- ⬤ **Car doors opening suddenly**
- ⬤ **Children running out from between vehicles**
- ◯ Glare from the sun
- ◯ Lack of road markings
- ◯ The headlights on parked cars being switched on
- ◯ Large goods vehicles

Approach and cross level crossings with care. Don't

- try to beat the barrier by driving through
- drive or ride onto the crossing unless the road is clear on the other side
- drive or ride nose-to-tail over it
- stop on or just over the crossing

Stop before the barrier and wait patiently.

When driving or riding on roads where there are many parked vehicles you must take extra care. Always be ready for the unexpected and drive or ride accordingly.

Children are small and you might not be able to see them about to emerge from between cars. Drivers may be getting in and out of their vehicles, providing another potential hazard. If the road is narrow, as it is in this picture, you will also need to look well down the road. This will help you to deal with any oncoming traffic safely.

Question

What is the main hazard a driver should be aware of when following this cyclist?

Mark one answer

- ⬤ **The cyclist may swerve out into the road**
- ⭕ The cyclist may move into the left gap and dismount
- ⭕ The contents of the cyclist's carrier may fall onto the road
- ⭕ The cyclist may wish to turn right at the end of the road

When following a cyclist be aware that they also have to deal with the hazards around them. They may wobble or swerve to avoid a pot-hole in the road. They might see a potential hazard and change direction suddenly.

Don't drive or ride very close to them or rev your engine impatiently. This will only add to their perception of a hazard and may rush them into a dangerous decision.

Question

The driver of which car has caused a hazard?

Mark one answer

- ⬤ **Car A**
- ⭕ Car B
- ⭕ Car C
- ⭕ Car D

The driver of car A has forced the approaching vehicle to the right onto the hatch-marked area of the road. It has also blocked the view of the other vehicle trying to emerge.

When dealing with busy junctions consider the other road users around you. Your actions must not put any other driver or rider at risk.

Question

What is the main hazard the driver of the red car (arrowed) should be most aware of?

You should try to anticipate the actions of the other road users around you. The driver of the red car should have made a mental note that the bus was at the bus stop. If you do this you will be prepared for the bus pulling out. Look and see how many more passengers are waiting to board. If the last one has just got on, the bus is likely to move off.

Mark one answer

● **The bus may move out into the road**
○ Glare from the sun may affect the driver's vision
○ The black car may stop suddenly
○ Oncoming vehicles will assume the driver is turning right

Question

In heavy motorway traffic you are being followed closely by the vehicle behind.
How can you lower the risk of an accident?

On a busy motorway traffic might still travel at high speeds although the weight of traffic means the vehicles are close together. Don't follow too close to the vehicle in front. If a driver behind seems to be 'pushing' you, increase your distance from the car in front by easing off the accelerator. This will lessen the risk of an accident involving several vehicles.

Mark one answer

● **Increase your distance from the vehicle in front**
○ Tap your foot on the brake pedal
○ Switch on your hazard lights
○ Move on to the hard shoulder and stop

Question

To drive you must be able to read a number plate from what distance?

Mark one answer

● **20.5 metres (67 feet)**
○ 10 metres (33 feet)
○ 15 metres (49 feet)
○ 205 metres (673 feet)

Question

You find that you need glasses to read vehicle number plates.
When must you wear them?

Mark one answer

● **At all times when driving**
○ Only in bad weather conditions
○ Only when you think it necessary
○ Only in bad light or at night time

Question

A driver can only read a number plate at the required distance with glasses on.
The glasses should be worn

Mark one answer

● **all the time when driving**
○ only when driving long distances
○ only when reversing
○ only in poor visibility

Question

You are about to drive home.
You cannot find the glasses you need to wear when driving.
You should

Mark one answer

● **find a way of getting home without driving**
○ drive home slowly, keeping to quiet roads
○ borrow a friend's glasses and drive home
○ drive home at night, so that the lights will help you

When you take your practical test your examiner will ask you to read a number plate from a distance of 20.5 metres (67 feet). This is a legal requirement to ensure that you see situations around you on the road.

Give yourself an eyesight test before you start your practical training. Then, throughout your driving life make periodical checks to ensure that your eyes have not deteriorated.

You might find you need glasses or contact lenses to read number plates. This is fine, but you must then wear them when you drive or ride.

Don't be tempted to drive if you have lost or forgotten your glasses. It is an obvious statement that you must be able to see clearly when driving.

Question
Which THREE result from drinking alcohol and driving?

Mark three answers

- 🔴 **Less control**
- 🔴 **False sense of confidence**
- 🔴 **Poor judgement of speed**
- ⭕ Faster reactions
- ⭕ Greater awareness of danger

Question
What are THREE ways that drinking alcohol can affect driving?

Mark three answers

- 🔴 **It slows down your reactions**
- 🔴 **It reduces your co-ordination**
- 🔴 **It affects your judgement of speed**
- ⭕ It reduces your confidence

Question
Which THREE of these are likely effects of drinking alcohol on driving?

Mark three answers

- 🔴 **Reduced co-ordination**
- 🔴 **Increased confidence**
- 🔴 **Poor judgement**
- ⭕ Increased concentration
- ⭕ Faster reactions
- ⭕ Colour blindness

Question
How does alcohol affect your driving?

Mark one answer ✓

- 🔴 **It reduces your concentration**
- ⭕ It speeds up your reactions
- ⭕ It increases your awareness
- ⭕ It improves your co-ordination

Alcohol will reduce your ability to drive or ride safely. Alcohol will

- reduce co-ordination
- slow down reactions
- affect judgement of speed

Drivers who drink before driving or riding are responsible for numerous deaths on our roads. One death is too many.

Alcohol can increase confidence to a point where a driver or rider's behaviour might become 'out of character'. Someone who normally behaves sensibly suddenly takes risks and enjoys it. Never let yourself get into this situation. Concentration and good judgement at all times are needed to be a good, safe driver.

Question

When driving, what is the maximum **legal** level for alcohol in your blood?

Mark one answer

● **80 mg per 100 ml**
○ 50 mg per 100 ml
○ 60 mg per 100 ml
○ 90 mg per 100 ml

Question

Which one of the following is NOT affected by alcohol?

Mark one answer

● **Perception of colours**
○ Judgement of speed
○ Reaction time
○ Co-ordination

Question

What advice should you give to a driver who has had a few alcoholic drinks at a party?

Mark one answer

● **Go home by public transport**
○ Have a strong cup of coffee and then drive home
○ Drive home carefully and slowly
○ Wait a short while and then drive home

Question

A driver attends a social event.
What precaution should the driver take?

Mark one answer

● **Avoid drinking alcohol completely**
○ Drink plenty of coffee after drinking alcohol
○ Avoid busy roads after drinking alcohol
○ Avoid drinking alcohol on an empty stomach

Question

You are about to drive but you feel ill.
You should

Mark one answer

● **not drive**
○ take suitable medicine before driving
○ shorten the journey if you can
○ promise yourself an early night

The maximum legal level for alcohol in your blood is 80 mg per 100 ml.

By the time you get to know how much alcohol you have in your blood it might be too late. It will probably mean you have been asked to give a sample to the police.

If you are going out, and intend to drive or ride, the safest option is not to drink alcohol at all. Enjoy yourself, but if you do drink, don't drive or ride.

Drinking black coffee or waiting a few hours will not make any difference. Alcohol takes time to leave the body. You might even be unfit to drive or ride the following morning.

It is most important that you are fit to drive or ride, and that bad health does not impair your judgement. Even a cold can make you unsafe to drive or ride. If you are feeling tired or unwell don't drive at all.

DSA THEORY TEST for cars and motorcycles

Question
Your doctor has given you a course of medicine.
Why should you ask if it is OK to drive?

Mark one answer

● Some types of medicine can cause your reactions to slow down

○ Drugs make you a better driver by quickening your reactions

○ You will have to let your insurance company know about the medicine

○ The medicine you take may affect your eyesight

Always check the label of any container you are about to take medication from. The contents might affect your driving.

Question
You are not sure if your cough medicine will affect your driving.
What TWO things could you do?

Mark two answers

● Ask your doctor

● Check the medicine label

○ Drive if you feel alright

○ Ask a friend or relative for advice

If you are taking medicine or drugs prescribed by your doctor check to ensure that it will not make you drowsy. If you forget to ask at the time of your visit to the surgery, check with your pharmacist.

Question
You take some cough medicine given to you by a friend.
What must you do before driving?

Mark one answer

● Check the label to see if the medicine will affect your driving

○ Drink some strong coffee

○ Ask your friend if taking the medicine affected their driving

○ Make a short journey to see if the medicine is affecting your driving

Never drive or ride having taken drugs you don't know about. They might affect your judgement and perception, and therefore endanger lives.

Question

You are taking drugs which are likely to affect your driving.
What should you do?

Mark one answer

● **Seek medical advice before driving**
○ Limit your driving to essential journeys
○ Only drive if accompanied by a full licence holder
○ Drive only for short distances

Check with your doctor or pharmacist if you think that the drugs you are taking are likely to make you feel drowsy.

Question

If you are feeling tired it is best to stop as soon as you can.
Until then you should

Mark one answer

● **ensure a supply of fresh air**
○ increase your speed to find a stopping place quickly
○ gently tap the steering wheel
○ keep changing speed to improve concentration

If you are travelling on a long journey plan your route before you leave. This will help you to

• be decisive at intersections and junctions
• plan your rest stops
• know approximately how long the journey will take

Question

If you start to feel tired on your journey you should

Mark one answer ✓

● **stop and have a short nap or some strong coffee**
○ stop and eat a large meal
○ stop immediately and take deep breaths
○ complete the journey, then have a good sleep

Make sure the vehicle you are travelling in is well ventilated. A warm, stuffy atmosphere can make you drowsy, which will impair your judgement and perception.

If you do feel yourself becoming tired, stop and take a break. Don't start your journey again until you feel refreshed.

Driving on a motorway for long distances is very tiring. If your journey involves several miles of motorway plan to stop before you become tired. Don't be tempted to miss out planned stops in order to complete your journey quicker.

Question
You are driving on a motorway.
You feel tired.
You should

Mark one answer
- ⬤ **leave the motorway at the next exit**
- ⵔ carry on but drive slowly
- ⵔ complete your journey as quickly as possible
- ⵔ stop on the hard shoulder

Question
How often should you stop on a long journey?

Mark one answer
- ⬤ **At least every two hours**
- ⵔ When you need petrol
- ⵔ At least every four hours
- ⵔ When you need to eat

Question
Which TWO things would help keep you alert during a long journey?

Mark two answers
- ⬤ **Make sure you get plenty of fresh air**
- ⬤ **Make regular stops for refreshments**
- ⵔ Finish your journey as fast as you can
- ⵔ Keep off the motorways and use country roads

If you do feel tired and there is no service station for many miles, leave the motorway at the next exit.

If you are travelling a long distance plan your journey carefully. Ensure you plan rest stops too so that you don't become tired. Make the rest stops about two hours apart. This will also help prevent any passengers becoming restless and possibly distracting you.

Your judgement and perception will be affected if you are not alert. Tiredness could endanger your passengers and other road users as well as yourself.

Make sure the vehicle you are driving is well ventilated. A warm, stuffy atmosphere will make you feel drowsy. Open a window or turn down the heating.

GOOD EGG

Puddleworth
Services ½m

Petrol

Question
Which should you do to help keep you alert during a long journey?

Mark one answer

● **Make regular stops for refreshments**
○ Finish your journey as fast as you can
○ Keep off the motorways and use country roads
○ Keep your helmet visor up

Question
You should NOT drive if

Mark one answer

● **you feel tired or unwell**
○ you suffer from cramps
○ you suffer from hay fever
○ you have just passed your test

Question
Which THREE are likely to make you lose concentration while driving?

Mark three answers

● **Looking at road maps**
● **Listening to loud music**
● **Using a mobile phone**
○ Using your windscreen washers
○ Looking in your wing mirror

Question
You have not worn suitable riding gear and get cold and wet when riding.
Which TWO are likely effects?

Mark two answers

● **You may lose concentration**
● **Your reaction times may slow**
○ Your visor may freeze up
○ You may slide off the seat
○ Your helmet may loosen

Before you drive or ride you must ensure that you

• are fit and well
• have planned your route
• have planned your rest stops

Looking at road maps while driving is very dangerous. If you are not sure of your route stop in a safe place and check the map. You must not allow anything to take your attention away from the road.

If you wish to use a mobile phone, stop in a safe place before doing so. If you use a mobile phone frequently have a 'hands free' phone fitted in your vehicle.

When driving or riding you must not allow anything to impair your awareness of any hazards.

If you are riding a motorcycle you should ensure that you are wearing suitable clothing. If you become cold and uncomfortable this could cause you to lose concentration.

Question

A driver pulls out of a side road in front of you. You have to brake hard. You should

Mark one answer

- ● **ignore the error and stay calm**
- ○ flash your lights to show your annoyance
- ○ sound your horn to show your annoyance
- ○ overtake as soon as possible

Question

Another driver does something that upsets you. You should

Mark one answer

- ● **try not to react**
- ○ let them know how you feel
- ○ flash your headlamps several times
- ○ sound your horn

If you are driving or riding where there are a number of side roads be alert. Drivers approaching or emerging from the side road might not be able to see you. Be especially careful if there are a lot of parked vehicles. If a vehicle does emerge and you have to stop quickly

- try to be tolerant
- learn from the experience

There are occasions when other drivers or riders make a misjudgement or a mistake. If this happens try not to let it worry you. Don't react by showing anger. Sounding the horn, flashing the headlamps or shouting at the other driver will not help the situation. Good anticipation will help to prevent these incidents becoming accidents.

This section looks at the risks when dealing with vulnerable road users.

The questions will ask you about

- Pedestrians
- Children
- Elderly drivers
- Disabled people
- Cyclists
- Motorcyclists
- Animals
- New drivers

Question
You should not ride too closely behind a lorry because

Mark one answer
- it will reduce your view ahead
- you will breathe in the lorry's exhaust fumes
- wind from the lorry will slow you down
- drivers behind you may not be able to see you

Question
You are riding along a main road with many side roads.
Why should you be particularly careful?

Mark one answer
- Drivers coming out from side roads may not see you
- Gusts of wind from the side roads may push you off course
- The road will be more slippery where cars have been turning
- Drivers will be travelling slowly when they approach a junction

Question
You are driving on a country road.
What should you expect to see coming towards you on YOUR side of the road?

Mark one answer
- Pedestrians
- Motorcycles
- Bicycles
- Horse riders

If you are following a large vehicle your view beyond it will be restricted. Drop back. This will help you to see more of the road ahead.

If you are riding along a main road where there are many side roads be alert. Drivers approaching or emerging from the side road may not be able to see you. Be especially careful if there are a lot of parked vehicles.

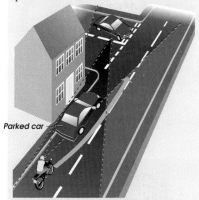

Parked car

Always drive at a speed that will enable you to slow down and stop in good time. If you look well ahead and anticipate the actions of other road users you will avoid having to brake suddenly or harshly.

On a quiet country road always be aware that there may be a hazard just around the next bend, such as a slow-moving vehicle or pedestrians. There might not be a pavement and people may be walking on your side of the road.

Question

Which sign means there may be people walking along the road?

Mark one answer

○

○

○

Question

You are turning left into a side road. Pedestrians are crossing the road near the junction.
You must

Mark one answer

● **wait for them to cross**
○ wave them on
○ sound your horn
○ switch on your hazard lights

Always check the road signs as you drive. They will keep you informed of hazards ahead and help you to anticipate any problems.

There are different types of signs showing pedestrians. Learn the meaning of each one. This will help you to be aware of the hazard ahead.

DSA THEORY TEST **for cars and motorcycles**

Question

You are turning left at a junction.
Pedestrians have started to cross the road.
You should

Mark one answer

● **give way to them**
○ go on, giving them plenty of room
○ stop and wave at them to cross
○ blow your horn and proceed

Question

You are turning left from a main road into a side road.
People are already crossing the road into which you are turning.
You should

Mark one answer

● **wait and allow them to cross**
○ continue, as it is your right of way
○ signal to them to continue crossing
○ sound your horn to warn them of your presence

If you are turning into a side road you should give way to pedestrians already crossing. They have priority. Don't

- wave them across the road
- sound the horn
- flash your lights
- give any other misleading signal – other road users may misinterpret your signal and you might lead the pedestrian into a dangerous situation.

If a pedestrian is slow or indecisive be patient and wait. Don't hurry them across by revving the engine.

Question

You are at a road junction, turning into a minor road.
There are pedestrians crossing the minor road.
You should

Mark one answer

- ● **give way to the pedestrians who are already crossing**
- ○ stop and wave the pedestrians across
- ○ sound your horn to let the pedestrians know you are there
- ○ carry on, the pedestrians should give way to you

Question

You are about to reverse into a side road.
A pedestrian wishes to cross behind you.
You should

Mark one answer

- ● **give way to the pedestrian**
- ○ wave to the pedestrian to stop
- ○ wave to the pedestrian to cross
- ○ reverse before the pedestrian starts to cross

Question

You want to turn right from a junction but your view is restricted by parked vehicles.
What should you do?

Mark one answer

- ● **Stop, then move slowly forward until you have a clear view**
- ○ Move out quickly, but be prepared to stop
- ○ Sound your horn and pull out if there is no reply
- ○ Stop, get out and look along the main road to check

Give way to pedestrians who are crossing a road you wish to turn into. Be considerate but don't wave or signal at them to cross.

If you need to reverse into a side road try to find a place which is free from traffic and pedestrians.

Practise good all-round observation before and during the manoeuvre. Always stop and give way to any pedestrians that wish to cross behind you. Don't

- wave them across the road
- sound the horn
- flash your lights
- give any other misleading signal – other road users may not have seen your signal and you may lead the pedestrian into a dangerous situation

If you want to turn right from a junction and your view is restricted STOP. Ease forward until you can see – there might be something approaching.

IF YOU DON'T KNOW, DON'T GO.

Question
In which THREE places would parking your vehicle cause danger or obstruction to other road users?

Mark three answers

- ● **In front of a property entrance**
- ● **At or near a bus stop**
- ● **On the approach to a level crossing**
- ○ On your driveway
- ○ In a marked parking space

Question
When you park your vehicle you must NOT

Mark one answer

- ● **obstruct other road users**
- ○ park on a major road
- ○ leave it in gear
- ○ leave the sidelights on

Question
The approach to a zebra crossing is marked with zigzag lines.
Which TWO must you NOT do within the marked area?

Mark two answers

- ● **Overtake**
- ● **Park**
- ○ Cross the lines
- ○ Drive at more than 10 mph

Don't park your vehicle where parking restrictions apply. Think carefully before you slow down and stop. Look at road markings and signs to ensure that you are not parking illegally.

Other road users such as lorries and buses need more room on the road, so don't park where your vehicle could cause an obstruction.

The Highway Code gives you full information on where and when you **cannot** park. Study this carefully and think about the reasons why the restrictions apply.

The approach to a pedestrian crossing is marked with zigzag lines. Parking here will

- block the view for pedestrians wishing to cross the road
- restrict drivers' or riders' view of the crossing

When you are approaching a pedestrian crossing don't overtake. The pedestrians waiting to cross the road might not see you as you pull alongside the leading vehicle.

Only stop on a pedestrian crossing if it is to avoid an accident. The crossing should be accessible for pedestrians at all times.

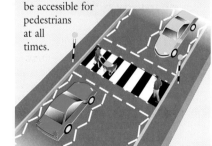

Question
When may you stop on a pedestrian crossing?

Mark one answer
- ● **To avoid an accident**
- ○ Not at any time
- ○ When there is a queue of traffic in front of you
- ○ Between the hours of 11 pm and 7 am

Question
Look at this picture. What is the danger you should be most aware of?

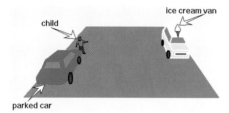

Mark one answer
- ● **The child may run out into the road**
- ○ The ice cream van may move off
- ○ The driver of the ice cream van may get out
- ○ The car on the left may move off

Question
You are driving past a line of parked cars. You notice a ball bouncing out into the road ahead. What should you do?

Mark one answer
- ● **Slow down and be prepared to stop for children**
- ○ Continue driving at the same speed and sound your horn
- ○ Continue driving at the same speed and flash your headlights
- ○ Stop and wave the children across to fetch their ball

Don't stop directly on a pedestrian crossing. If you are moving in a queue look well ahead and try to judge the flow of traffic. Leave a gap for pedestrians to cross.

Extra care must be taken when there are children about. Look out for them at all times but especially

- in residential areas
- near parks
- near schools

Where there are crossing places used by children be extra cautious. Don't

- overtake
- drive at high speed

If you see an ice cream van ask yourself, 'Where are the children?' They might run across the road to it. Their small size may prevent you seeing them emerging from behind parked vehicles.

Beware of children playing in the street and running out into the road. If a ball bounces out from the pavement slow down and stop. Don't encourage anyone to retrieve it. Other road users may not see your signal and you might lead a child into a dangerous situation.

Question
What does this sign warn you to look for?

Mark one answer
- ● **School children**
- ○ A school crossing patrol
- ○ A pedestrian crossing
- ○ A park

Question
How will a school crossing patrol signal you to stop?

Mark one answer
- ● **By displaying a stop sign**
- ○ By pointing to children on the opposite pavement
- ○ By displaying a red light
- ○ By giving you an arm signal

Question
You see someone step onto the road holding this sign.
What must you do?

Mark one answer
- ● **Pull up before the person**
- ○ Slow down and look out for children
- ○ Signal the person to cross
- ○ Drive carefully round the person

Look out for road signs as you drive. There could be a sign to warn you that children may be about. If you are driving near a school take extra care, as children can be impulsive and might dart out into the road without warning. Drive at an appropriate speed and try to anticipate their actions.

If someone steps out into the road with a school crossing sign you must stop. Don't

- wave anyone across the road
- get impatient or rev your engine

Check the road signs as you drive. If you see a sign for a school there might be a school crossing patrol ahead, especially if amber flashing lights show beneath it.

Question
A school crossing patrol shows a stop children sign.
What must you do?

Mark one answer
● **Stop at all times**
○ Continue if safe to do so
○ Slow down and be ready to stop
○ Stop ONLY if children are crossing

Question
You are approaching a school crossing patrol.
When this sign is held up you must

Mark one answer
● **stop and allow any children to cross**
○ stop and beckon the children to cross
○ stop only if the children are on a pedestrian crossing
○ stop only when the children are actually crossing the road

Question
You are following a car driven by an elderly driver.
You should

Mark one answer
● **be aware that the driver's reactions may not be as fast as yours**
○ expect the driver to drive badly
○ flash your lights and overtake
○ stay close behind and drive carefully

You must show consideration to other road users. Their reactions may be slower and they might need more time to deal with a situation. Be tolerant and don't lose patience or show your annoyance.

DSA THEORY TEST for cars and motorcycles

Question
You see a pedestrian carrying a white stick.
This shows that the person is

Mark one answer

- ● **blind**
- ○ disabled
- ○ deaf
- ○ elderly

If you see a pedestrian carrying a white stick it will mean the person is partially sighted or blind. Make allowances for their hesitation at crossings or junctions.

Question
You see a pedestrian with a white stick and two red reflective bands.
This means the person is

Mark one answer

- ● **deaf and blind**
- ○ physically disabled
- ○ deaf and dumb
- ○ blind and dumb

If the person is also deaf the stick will have two red reflective bands. You can't tell if a pedestrian is deaf – don't assume everyone can hear you approaching.

Question
You are driving behind a cyclist.
You wish to turn left just ahead.
You should

When driving or riding make allowances for cyclists. Allow them plenty of room. If you are following a cyclist be aware that they also have to deal with hazards around them. They might swerve or change direction suddenly to avoid an uneven road surface.

Mark one answer

- ● **hold back until the cyclist has passed the junction**
- ○ overtake the cyclist before the junction
- ○ pull alongside the cyclist and stay level until after the junction
- ○ go around the cyclist on the junction

Question
You should NEVER attempt to overtake a cyclist

Mark one answer

- ● **just before you turn left**
- ○ just before you turn right
- ○ on a one-way street
- ○ on a dual carriageway

If you want to turn left and there is a cyclist in front of you, hold back. Wait until the cyclist has passed the junction and then turn left behind them.

Question
You are coming up to a roundabout.
A cyclist is signalling to turn right.
What should you do?

Mark one answer
- ● **Give the cyclist plenty of room**
- ○ Overtake on the right
- ○ Give a horn warning
- ○ Signal the cyclist to move across

If you are following a cyclist who is signalling to turn right at a roundabout leave plenty of room. Give them space and time to get into the correct lane.

Question
You are driving behind two cyclists.
They approach a roundabout in the left-hand lane.
In which direction should you expect the cyclists to go?

Mark one answer
- ● **Any direction**
- ○ Left
- ○ Right
- ○ Straight ahead

If you are following a cyclist into a roundabout be aware of them as they might not be taking the exit you anticipate. If they are turning right they may not have been able to get into the correct lane due to the heavy traffic. Cyclists approaching in the left–hand lane may be turning right. Give them room.

Question
You are approaching the roundabout and see the cyclist signal right.
Why is the cyclist keeping to the left?

Mark one answer
- ● **The cyclist is slower and more vulnerable**
- ○ It is a quicker route for the cyclist
- ○ The cyclist is going to turn left instead
- ○ The cyclist thinks *The Highway Code* does not apply to bicycles

Cycling in today's heavy traffic can be hazardous. Some cyclists may not feel happy about crossing the path of traffic to take up a position in an outside lane. Be aware of this and understand that, although in the left–hand lane, the cyclist might be turning right.

Question
When you are overtaking a cyclist you should leave as much room as you would give to a car. Why is this?

Mark one answer
- ● **The cyclist might swerve**
- ○ The cyclist might change lanes
- ○ The cyclist might get off the bike
- ○ The cyclist might have to make a right turn

If you intend to overtake a cyclist look at the road ahead. Check if the cyclist needs to change direction for a parked vehicle or an uneven road surface. When you have a safe place to overtake leave as much room as you would for a car. Don't cut in sharply or pass too closely.

Question
You are overtaking a motorcyclist.
What should you do?

Mark one answer
- ● **Give as much room as you would for a car**
- ○ Try to pass on a bend
- ○ Move over to the opposite side of the road
- ○ Pass close by and as quickly as possible

Question
Which TWO should you allow extra room when overtaking? ✓

Mark two answers
- ● **Motorcycles**
- ● **Bicycles**
- ○ Tractors
- ○ Road-sweeping vehicles

Question
Why should you allow extra room when overtaking a motorcyclist on a windy day?

Mark one answer
- ● **The rider may be blown across in front of you**
- ○ The rider may turn off suddenly to get out of the wind
- ○ The rider may stop suddenly
- ○ The rider may be travelling faster than normal

Question
You are waiting to come out of a side road. Why should you watch carefully for motorcycles?

Mark one answer
- ● **Motorcycles are small and hard to see**
- ○ Motorcycles are usually faster than cars
- ○ Police patrols often use motorcycles
- ○ Motorcycles have right of way

If you are following a motorcycle and you wish to overtake look well ahead. You will need as much room to pass it as you would a car. You also have the added risk of the rider swerving or changing direction due to an uneven road surface.

Don't pass riders too closely as this may cause them to lose balance. Always leave as much room as you would for a car, and don't cut in.

A motorcyclist's position on the road can be affected by high winds. If you are driving or riding on a windy day be aware that the conditions might force a motorcyclist to swerve or wobble. Take this into consideration if you are following or wish to overtake.

If you are waiting to emerge from a side road watch out for motorcyclists. They are smaller and more difficult to see. Be especially careful if there are parked vehicles restricting your view. There might be a motorcyclist appoaching.

IF YOU DON'T KNOW, DON'T GO.

Question

Where should you take **particular** care to look out for motorcyclists and cyclists?

Mark one answer

- ● At junctions
- ○ On dual carriageways
- ○ At zebra crossings
- ○ On one-way streets

Question

Where **in particular** should you look out for motorcyclists?

Mark one answer

- ● At a road junction
- ○ In a filling station
- ○ Near a service area
- ○ When entering a car park

Question

You are driving in town.
There is a bus at the bus stop on the other side of the road.
Why should you be careful? ✓

Mark one answer

- ● Pedestrians may come from behind the bus
- ○ The bus may have broken down
- ○ The bus may move off suddenly
- ○ The bus may remain stationary

Question

Which THREE should you do when passing sheep on a road?

Mark three answers

- ● Allow plenty of room
- ● Drive very slowly
- ● Be ready to stop
- ○ Pass quickly but quietly
- ○ Briefly sound your horn

Motorcyclists and cyclists may be more difficult to see on the road. This is especially the case at junctions. You may not be able to see a motorcyclist approaching a junction if your view is blocked by other traffic. Be aware of the possibility. A motorcycle may be travelling as fast as a car, or faster. Make sure you judge speeds correctly before you emerge.

Always look ahead and try to make use of the information you see. This will enable you to anticipate possible hazards, and give you more time to deal with them as they occur.

If you see a bus ahead watch out for pedestrians. They may cross from behind it.

If you see animals in the road ahead slow down and be ready to stop. Animals are easily frightened by

- noise
- vehicles passing too close to them

Stop if signalled to by the person in charge. Switch off your engine if the animals are taking a long time to clear the road.

Question

How should you overtake horse riders?

Mark one answer

● **Drive slowly and leave plenty of room**

○ Drive up close and overtake as soon as possible

○ Speed is not important but allow plenty of room

○ Use your horn just once to warn them

Question

When passing animals you should NOT

Mark one answer

● **rev the engine or sound the horn**

○ change down to a lower gear

○ use your direction indicators

○ have any lights on

Question

You notice horse riders in front.
What should you do FIRST?

Mark one answer

● **Be prepared to slow down**

○ Pull out to the middle of the road

○ Accelerate around them

○ Signal right

Question

As you are driving along you meet a group of horses and riders from a riding school.
Why should you be extra cautious?

Mark one answer

● **Many of the riders may be learners**

○ They will be moving in single file

○ They will be moving slowly

○ The horses will panic more because they are in a group

If you are driving or riding on a country road then take extra care. Be ready for

- farm animals
- horses
- pedestrians
- farm vehicles

Always be prepared to slow down or stop.

When you are driving or riding you must always look well ahead and be ready to deal with hazards as they occur. If you see a group of horses ahead be extra cautious, especially if they are being ridden by children. The riders might be learners and may not be able to control the animal if it is startled. Approach

- slowly and quietly
- without revving the engine
- without sounding the horn

When you do overtake them do so at a safe place and give them plenty of room.

Question
You are driving on a narrow country road.
Where would you find it most difficult to see
horses and riders ahead of you?

Mark one answer

● **On left-hand bends**
○ When travelling downhill
○ When travelling uphill
○ On right-hand bends

Question
A horse rider is in the left lane approaching a
roundabout.
The driver behind should expect the rider to

Mark one answer

● **go in any direction**
○ turn right
○ turn left
○ go ahead

Question
What lane will horse riders take when going
round a roundabout?

Mark one answer

● **Left**
○ Right
○ Centre
○ Between centre and right

Question
Which age group is most likely to be involved in a
road accident?

Mark one answer

● **17 to 25 year-olds**
○ 36 to 45 year-olds
○ 55 year-olds and over
○ 46 to 55 year-olds

Question
What is the most common factor in causing road
accidents?

Mark one answer

● **Driver error**
○ Weather conditions
○ Road conditions
○ Mechanical failure

You are more likely to see horses on
country roads. As these roads can be
narrow extra care must be taken when
approaching left-hand bends. Your view
of the road ahead will be restricted.

Horses and their riders will move more
slowly than other road users. They might
not have time to cut across busy traffic
to take up positions in the offside lane.
For this reason a horse and rider may
approach a roundabout in the left-hand
lane, even though they are turning right.
You must be aware of this and leave
them plenty of room. Don't

• sound your horn
• rev your engine
• drive too close

Every effort must be made to ensure
that the animals are not startled or
frightened.

Statistics show that if you are between
the ages of 17 and 25 you are more
likely to be involved in a road accident.
There are several reasons contributing to
this but in most cases accidents are due
to driver or rider error.

Bad weather and different conditions
will increase the risks so you must drive
accordingly.

Be aware of the distance it will take you
to stop

• in good conditions
• during wet or icy weather
• when you are tired
• when you don't concentrate or are
  distracted. (Your thinking distance
  will increase.)

DSA THEORY TEST for cars and motorcycles

Question
You have just passed your driving test. How likely are you to have an accident, compared with other drivers?

Mark one answer
- ● More likely
- ○ It depends on your age
- ○ Less likely
- ○ About the same

Question
As a new driver, how can you decrease your risk of accidents on the motorway?

Mark one answer
- ● By taking further training
- ○ By keeping up with the car in front
- ○ By never driving over 45 mph
- ○ By driving only in the nearside lane

Question
Your vehicle hits a pedestrian at 40 mph. The pedestrian

Mark one answer
- ● will probably be killed
- ○ will certainly be killed
- ○ will certainly survive
- ○ will probably survive

When you pass your practical driving test you will have demonstrated that you are safe to drive or ride without supervision. It takes experience to become a good driver. Even then, try to learn from your experiences. This will increase your ability to anticipate the actions of other drivers and therefore help to make you a safer driver.

You are more likely to have an accident in the first year after taking your test. Lack of experience means you might not react to hazards as quickly as a more experienced driver or rider. Further training will help you to become safer on the roads.

If you are a motorcyclist ask your Compulsory Basic Training (CBT) instructor about this.

If you are a car driver ask your Approved Driving Instructor about the PASS PLUS scheme. This is a course designed to give you further instruction which includes driving

- in town
- out of town
- in all weathers
- at night
- on dual carriageways
- on motorways

Taking further training with a professional will help you to gain experience and positive driving skills. Taking the PASS PLUS course may also provide you with cheaper insurance.

Whether driving or riding you must always be aware that there may be others on the road who are particularly vulnerable. Always be on the lookout for danger and adjust your speed accordingly.

SECTION 7 OTHER TYPES OF VEHICLE

This section looks at the risks when dealing with different types of vehicle.

The questions will ask you about

- Motorcycles
- Lorries
- Buses

Question

The road is wet.
Why might a motorcyclist steer round drain covers on a bend?

Mark one answer

● **To prevent the motorcycle sliding on the metal drain covers**

○ To avoid puncturing the tyres on the edge of the drain covers

○ To help judge the bend using the drain covers as marker points

○ To avoid splashing pedestrians on the pavement

Question

Motorcyclists are more vulnerable than car drivers because they

Mark one answer

● **are affected more by changes in road surface**

○ ride at higher speeds

○ take corners at higher speeds

○ can accelerate faster than cars

Question

It is very windy.
You are behind a motorcyclist who is overtaking a high-sided vehicle.
What should you do?

Mark one answer

● **Keep well back**

○ Overtake the motorcyclist immediately

○ Stay level with the motorcyclist

○ Keep close to the motorcyclist

The actions other drivers take may be due to the size or characteristics of their vehicle. If you understand this it will help you to anticipate their actions.

Motorcyclists will be checking the road ahead for uneven or slippery surfaces, especially in wet weather. They may need to move across their lane to avoid road surface hazards such as

- metal drain covers
- tar banding
- wet leaves or mud
- oily patches

Motorcyclists are affected more by windy weather than other vehicles. Keep well back as they could be be blown off course.

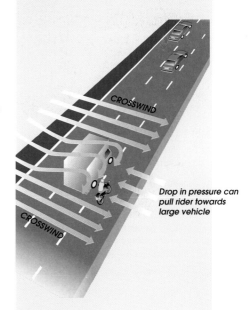

CROSSWIND

CROSSWIND

Drop in pressure can pull rider towards large vehicle

Question
You are following a large articulated vehicle.
It is going to turn left into a narrow road.
What action should you take?

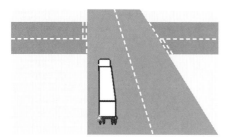

Lorries are larger and longer than other vehicles. This will affect their position when approaching junctions – especially when turning left.

Approaching a left turn a lorry may swing out to the right. This is to allow the rear wheels to clear the kerb as it turns. If you see a gap on the nearside don't try to filter through.

Mark one answer
- ● **Be prepared to stop behind**
- ○ Move out and overtake on the offside
- ○ Pass on the left as the vehicle moves out
- ○ Overtake quickly before the lorry moves out

Question
You are following a long vehicle.
It approaches a crossroads and signals left, but moves out to the right.
You should

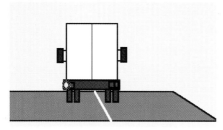

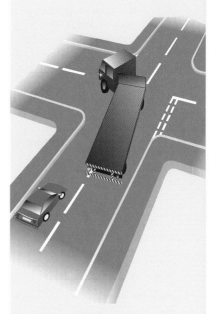

Mark one answer
- ● **stay well back and give it room**
- ○ get closer in order to pass it quickly
- ○ assume the signal is wrong and it is really turning right
- ○ overtake as it starts to slow down

Question
You are following a long vehicle approaching a crossroads.
The driver signals right but moves close to the left-hand kerb.
What should you do?

When a long vehicle is going to turn right it may need to keep close to the left-hand kerb. This is to prevent the rear end of the vehicle or trailer cutting the corner. You need to be aware of how long vehicles behave in such situations.

Don't overtake the lorry because it could turn as you are alongside. Stay behind and give it plenty of room.

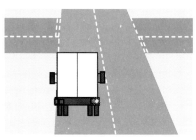

Mark one answer
- ● **Wait behind the long vehicle**
- ○ Warn the driver of wrong signal
- ○ Report the driver to the police
- ○ Overtake on the right-hand side

Question
You are approaching a mini-roundabout.
The long vehicle in front is signalling left but positioned over to the right.
You should

At mini-roundabouts there is not much room for a long vehicle to manoeuvre. It will have to swing out wide so that it can complete the turn safely. Keep well back and allow plenty of room.

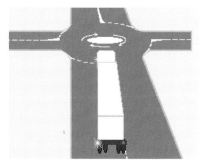

Mark one answer
- ● **keep well back**
- ○ sound your horn
- ○ overtake on the left
- ○ follow the same course as the lorry

Question

Before overtaking a large vehicle you should keep well back.

Why is this?

✓

Mark one answer

⬤ **To get the best view of the road ahead**

○ To give acceleration space to overtake quickly on blind bends

○ To leave a gap in case the vehicle stops and rolls back

○ To offer other drivers a safe gap if they want to overtake you

Question

You wish to overtake a long, slow-moving vehicle on a busy road.

You should

Mark one answer

⬤ **keep well back until you can see it is clear**

○ wait behind until the driver waves you past

○ flash your headlights for the oncoming traffic to give way

○ follow it closely and keep moving out to see the road ahead

Question

When about to overtake a long vehicle you should

Mark one answer

⬤ **stay well back from the lorry to obtain a better view**

○ sound the horn to warn the driver you are there

○ drive close to the lorry in order to pass more quickly

○ flash your lights and wait for the driver to signal when it is safe

When following a large vehicle keep well back. If you are too close

- you will not be able to see the road ahead
- the driver of the long vehicle might not be able to see you in his mirrors

If you wish to overtake a long vehicle stay well back so that you can see the road ahead. Don't

- get up close to the vehicle – this will restrict your view of the road ahead
- get impatient – overtaking on a busy road calls for sound judgement
- take a gamble – only overtake when you can see that you can safely complete the manoeuvre
- flash your headlights – this could confuse and mislead other traffic
- sound your horn

If you are thinking about overtaking ask yourself if it is really necessary. An unladen large vehicle can make surprisingly good progress.

DSA THEORY TEST for cars and motorcycles

Question

The FIRST thing you should do when you want to overtake a large lorry is

Mark one answer

- **stay well back to get a better view**
- move close behind so you can pass quickly
- keep in close to the left-hand side
- flash your headlights and wait for the driver to wave you on

Question

Why is passing a lorry more risky than passing a car?

Mark one answer

- **Lorries are longer than cars**
- Lorries may suddenly pull up
- The brakes of lorries are not as good
- Lorries climb hills more slowly

When you are planning to overtake a large vehicle take its length into account. It will take you longer to pass a lorry or coach than another car. You will need to look further ahead.

Hazards to watch for include

- oncoming traffic
- junctions
- bends or dips which could restrict your view
- any signs or road markings prohibiting overtaking

Never begin to overtake unless you can see it is safe to complete the manoeuvre.

Question
When you approach a bus signalling to move off from a bus stop you should

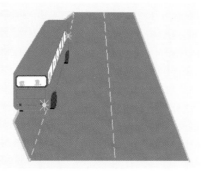

Mark one answer
- ● **allow it to pull away if safe**
- ○ get past before it moves
- ○ flash your headlamps as you approach
- ○ signal left and wave the bus on

Give way to buses whenever you can do so safely, especially when they signal to pull away from bus stops. Look out for people who have got off the bus and may try to cross the road. Don't

- try to accelerate past before it moves away
- flash your lights – other road users may be misled by this signal

Question
In which THREE places could a strong crosswind affect your course?

Mark three answers
- ● **After overtaking a large vehicle**
- ● **When passing gaps in hedges**
- ● **On exposed sections of roadway**
- ○ In towns
- ○ In tunnels
- ○ When passing parked vehicles

Crosswinds affect some vehicles more than others. The worst affected vehicles are

- high-sided vehicles
- caravans
- motorcycles
- cycles

It is important to be aware of which types of vehicles are affected so that you can anticipate their actions.

DSA THEORY TEST for cars and motorcycles

Question
Which of these vehicles is LEAST likely to be
affected by crosswinds?

Mark one answer

● **Cars**
○ Cyclists
○ Motorcyclists
○ High-sided vehicles

Question
You are following a large lorry on a wet road.
Spray makes it difficult to see.
You should

Mark one answer

● **drop back until you can see better**
○ put your headlights on full beam
○ keep close to the lorry, away from the spray
○ speed up and overtake quickly

Question
You are driving on a wet motorway with surface
spray.
You should

Mark one answer

● **use dipped headlights**
○ use your hazard flashers
○ use your rear fog lights
○ drive in any lane with no traffic

Crosswinds can take you by surprise

- after overtaking a large vehicle
- when passing gaps between
  hedges or buildings
- on exposed sections of road

Cars are affected by side winds but
to a lesser extent than other vehicles.

In the wet, large vehicles may throw up
a lot of spray. This will make it difficult
to see ahead. Dropping back further will

- move you out of the spray and so
  allow you to see further
- increase your separation distance.
  It takes longer to stop in the wet
  and you need to allow more room

Don't

- get up close behind
- overtake, unless you can see the way
  ahead is clear

When surface spray reduces visibility
switch on your dipped headlights. This
will help other road users to see you.

This section looks at the handling of your
vehicle in different conditions.

The questions will ask you about

- Weather conditions

- Road conditions

- The time of day

- Speed

- Traffic calming

Question

You shouldn't drive with your foot on the clutch for longer than necessary because it

Mark one answer

- ● **reduces your control of the vehicle**
- ○ increases wear on the gearbox
- ○ increases petrol consumption
- ○ reduces the grip of the tyres

Question

You shouldn't ride with your clutch in for longer than necessary because it

Mark one answer

- ● **reduces your control of the motorcycle**
- ○ increases wear on the gearbox
- ○ increases petrol consumption
- ○ reduces the grip of the tyres

Question

What are THREE main reasons why coasting downhill is wrong?

Mark three answers

- ● **The vehicle will pick up speed**
- ● **It could be difficult to get into gear**
- ● **You have less braking and steering control**
- ○ Petrol consumption will be higher
- ○ It puts more wear and tear on the tyres
- ○ It damages the engine

Question

Why is coasting wrong?

Mark one answer

- ● **There is no engine braking**
- ○ It will cause the car to skid
- ○ It will make the engine stall
- ○ The engine will run faster

You must have complete control of your vehicle or machine at all times.

Pressing down the clutch pedal or riding with the clutch in for longer than necessary is referred to as coasting. Coasting the vehicle or machine will

- cause the vehicle or machine to pick up speed
- give you less steering and braking control
- make selecting the correct gear difficult

If you are travelling downhill your vehicle or machine will gather speed quickly. The engine will not be able to assist the braking.

It is especially important that you don't coast your vehicle

- at junctions
- approaching hazards
- on bends

Try to look ahead and read the road. Plan your approach to junctions and select the correct gear in good time. This will give you the control you need to deal with any hazards that occur.

You will coast a little every time you change gear. This cannot be avoided but this should be kept to a minimum.

Question

Which THREE of the following will affect your stopping distance?

Mark three answers

- ● **How fast you are going**
- ● **The tyres on your vehicle**
- ● **The weather**
- ○ The time of day
- ○ The street lighting

Question

You are following a vehicle at a safe distance on a wet road.
Another driver overtakes you and pulls into the gap you had left.
What should you do?   ✓

Mark one answer

- ● **Drop back to regain a safe distance**
- ○ Flash your headlights as a warning
- ○ Try to overtake safely as soon as you can
- ○ Stay close to the other vehicle until it moves on

Question

You are driving in the left-hand lane of a dual carriageway.
Another vehicle overtakes and pulls in front of you leaving you without enough separation distance.
You should

Mark one answer

- ● **drop back**
- ○ move to the right lane
- ○ continue as you are
- ○ sound your horn

Always drive in accordance with the conditions. The weather will affect the way your vehicle or machine behaves. It will increase the time it takes for you to stop and can affect your control.

Drive at a speed that will allow you to stop safely and in good time.

Your stopping distance in wet weather will increase. You should double the separation distance from the car in front. Your tyres will have less grip on the road and therefore need more time to stop.

If another vehicle pulls into the gap you have left ease back until you have regained your stopping distance. Don't flash your lights or drive up close to it.

Dual carriageways have at least two lanes in each direction. There will be a central reserve where there may be a safety barrier.

If you are overtaken by another vehicle and it cuts in too closely don't react by flashing your lights or giving any other signal. Gradually increase your distance from the vehicle so that you have a safe gap if you need to stop.

DSA THEORY TEST for cars and motorcycles

Question

You wish to overtake on a dual carriageway. You see in your mirror that the car behind has pulled out to overtake you. You should

Mark one answer

● **not signal until the car has passed**

○ signal and pull out to overtake

○ signal to tell the driver behind that you also want to overtake

○ touch the brakes to show your brake lights

Before you overtake ask yourself, 'Is it really necessary?'

Look well ahead to check for hazards. Check in your mirror. If there is a vehicle about to overtake you wait until it has passed before you signal to pull out. Then do so safely.

Question

In which THREE of these situations may you overtake another vehicle on the left?

Mark three answers

● **When you are in a one-way street**

● **When the vehicle in front is signalling to turn right**

● **In slow-moving traffic queues when traffic in the right-hand lane is moving more slowly**

○ When approaching a motorway slip road where you will be turning off

○ When a slower vehicle is travelling in the right-hand lane of a dual carriageway

At certain times of the day traffic might be heavy. If traffic is moving in queues and vehicles in the right-hand lane are moving more slowly you may overtake on the left. Don't keep changing lanes to try and beat the queue.

You may also overtake on the left

• when the vehicle in front is signalling to turn right

• in a one-way street

Question

How should you drive around a bend on ice?

Mark one answer

● **Slowly and smoothly**

○ Using the clutch and brake together

○ In first gear

○ Braking as you enter the bend

When the weather is cold and the roads are icy you must be aware that your vehicle or machine will handle differently. The tyres will loose much of their grip on the road which will greatly affect your steering control. If you are driving around bends in icy weather do so slowly and smoothly.

Question
Which FOUR types of road surface increase the risk of skidding for motorcyclists?

Mark four answers

- White lining
- Tar banding
- Yellow grid lining
- Loose chippings
- Dry tarmac

Question
Which THREE of these can cause skidding?

Mark three answers

- Leaning too far over when cornering
- Braking too hard
- Changing direction suddenly
- Braking too gently
- Staying upright when cornering

Question
You are approaching a road with a surface of loose chippings.
What should you do?

Mark one answer

- Slow down
- Ride normally
- Speed up
- Stop

If you are riding a motorcycle you must look at the road surface ahead. The stability of your machine will depend on it. Look out for

- pot-holes
- loose surfaces and gravel
- drain covers (especially in the wet)
- oily surfaces
- road markings
- tar banding
- tram lines
- wet mud and leaves

In order to keep control of your vehicle and prevent skidding you must plan well ahead to prevent harsh, late braking. Take the road and weather conditions into consideration and ride accordingly. You should

- ride at an appropriate speed
- apply both front and rear brakes evenly
- brake when travelling in a straight line and your machine is upright

Don't make sudden changes of direction unless you are avoiding an accident.

The handling of your machine will be greatly affected by the road surface you are riding on. Look at the road ahead and be alert if the road looks uneven or has loose chippings. Slow down in good time – braking harshly here will cause you to skid.

DSA THEORY TEST for cars and motorcycles

Question
How can you best control your vehicle when driving in snow?

Mark one answer
- **By driving slowly in as high a gear as possible**
- By staying in low gear and gripping the steering wheel tightly
- By driving in first gear
- By keeping the engine revs high and slipping the clutch

Question
To correct a rear-wheel skid you should

Mark one answer
- **turn into it**
- not turn at all
- turn away from it
- apply your handbrake

Question
Why should you test your brakes after this hazard?

Mark one answer
- **Because your brakes would be soaking wet**
- Because you will be driving on a slippery road
- Because you would have driven down a long hill
- Because you would have just crossed a long bridge

If the ground is covered in snow move off in as high a gear as possible. This will lessen the chance of skidding by reducing the power driven to the wheels.

Prevention is better than cure so it is important that you take every precaution to prevent a skid. If you do feel your vehicle beginning to skid, try to steer to recover control. Don't brake suddenly – this will only make the situation worse.

A ford is a crossing over a stream which is shallow enough to drive through. If you have driven through a ford or a deep puddle the water can affect your brakes. Be sure you check they are working before returning to normal speed.

Question

You have to make a journey in fog.
What are the TWO most important things you
should do before you set out?

Mark two answers

- ● **Check your lights are working**
- ● **Make sure the windows are clean**
- ○ Top up the radiator with anti-freeze
- ○ Make sure you have a warning triangle in the vehicle
- ○ Check the battery

Don't drive in fog unless you really have to. If it is necessary for you to do so make sure

- • your lights are working
- • your windows and lights are clean

Question

You have to make a journey in fog.
What are the TWO most important things you
should do before you set out?

Mark two answers

- ● **Check your lights are working**
- ● **Make sure your visor is clean**
- ○ Fill up with fuel
- ○ Make sure you have a warm drink with you
- ○ Check the battery

If you are riding a motorcycle keep your visor as clean as possible to give you a clear view of the road. It is a good idea to carry a clean, damp cloth in a polythene bag for this purpose. When the weather is foggy or misty ensure that your lights are clean and can be seen clearly by other road users.

Question

You have to make a journey in foggy conditions.
You should

Mark one answer

- ● **leave plenty of time for your journey**
- ○ follow closely other vehicles' tail lights
- ○ never use de-misters and windscreen wipers
- ○ keep two seconds behind other vehicles

If you are planning to make a journey in foggy conditions listen to the weather reports on the radio or television. Don't drive if visibility is very low or your journey isn't necessary. If you do travel, leave plenty of time for your journey. If there is someone expecting you at the other end of your journey let them know you will be taking longer than normal to arrive. Take your time and don't hurry.

Question

You are following other vehicles in fog with your lights on.
How else can you reduce the chances of being involved in an accident?

Mark one answer

- ● **Reduce your speed and increase the gap**
- ○ Keep close to the vehicle in front
- ○ Use your main beam instead of dipped headlights
- ○ Keep together with the faster vehicles

Always ensure that you have your lights on and you are seen by all other road users. Use dipped headlights. If visibility is below 100 metres (330 feet) use fog lights and high-intensity rear lights. Drive at a sensible speed and don't follow too closely the car in front. You will need your stopping distance as the road is likely to be wet and slippery.

 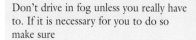

Question
Why should you always reduce your speed when driving in fog?

Mark one answer

● **Because it is more difficult to see events ahead**
○ Because the brakes do not work as well
○ Because you could be dazzled by other people's fog lights
○ Because the engine is colder

Driving in fog is hazardous. Only travel out if it is really necessary. To drive or ride safely you must always look well ahead. In fog this will not be possible and you will have less time to react to any hazards. You must reduce your speed.

Question
You are driving in fog.
The car behind seems to be very close.
You should

Mark one answer

● **continue cautiously**
○ switch on your hazard warning lights
○ pull over and stop immediately
○ speed up to get away

If the car behind seems to be too close to you the driver is probably using your rear lights as a guide through the fog. This is not advisable. A good separation distance will be even more important on a wet road surface. Don't react to this but continue cautiously.

Question
You are driving in fog.
Why should you keep well back from the vehicle in front?

Mark one answer

● **In case it stops suddenly**
○ In case it changes direction suddenly
○ In case its fog lights dazzle you
○ In case its brake lights dazzle you

If you are following another road user in fog stay well back. The driver in front will not be able to see hazards until late and might brake suddenly. You will need a good separation distance as the road surface is likely to be wet and slippery.

Question

You should switch your rear fog lights on when visibility drops below

Mark one answer

- ● **100 metres (330 feet)**
- ○ your overall stopping distance
- ○ ten car lengths
- ○ 10 metres (33 feet)

Question

You are driving in poor visibility.
You **can** see more than 100 metres (330 feet) ahead.
How can you make sure other drivers can see you?

Mark one answer

- ● **Turn on your dipped headlights**
- ○ Follow the vehicle in front closely
- ○ Turn on your rear fog lights
- ○ Keep well out towards the middle of the road

Question

You should only use rear fog lights when you cannot see further than about

Mark one answer

- ● **100 metres (330 feet)**
- ○ 200 metres (660 feet)
- ○ 250 metres (800 feet)
- ○ 150 metres (495 feet)

Question

You have to park on the road in fog.
You should

Mark one answer

- ● **leave sidelights on**
- ○ leave dipped headlights and fog lights on
- ○ leave dipped headlights on
- ○ leave main beam headlights on

If visibility drops below 100 metres (330 feet) you should switch on your rear fog lights. This will help other road users to see you.

Don't forget to turn them off once visibility is clear. The brightness of the fog lights might be mistaken for brake lights.

You should always use your headlights in fog. They should be on dipped beam to prevent the light reflecting back off the fog.

If you have to park your vehicle in foggy conditions it is important that it can be seen by other road users.

Try to find a place to park off the road. If this is not possible leave it facing in the same direction as the traffic. Make sure your lights are clean and that you leave your sidelights on.

DSA THEORY TEST for cars and motorcycles

Question
The best place to park your motorcycle is

Mark one answer
- ● **on firm, level ground**
- ○ on soft tarmac
- ○ on bumpy ground
- ○ on grass

If you are parking a motorcycle find a place where there is firm ground. Soft ground might cause the stand to sink and the bike to fall over. The ground should also be even and level to ensure that the bike is stable. If possible park your machine off the road.

Question
You are driving on a motorway in fog
The left-hand edge of the motorway can be identified by reflective studs.
What colour are they?

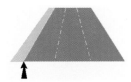

Mark one answer
- ● **Red**
- ○ Green
- ○ Amber
- ○ White

Be especially careful if you are driving on a motorway in fog. You must be able to stop well within the distance you can see to be clear. Keep in the left-hand lane. Reflective studs are used on motorways to help you in poor visibility. The studs are coloured so that you know which lane you are in and where slip roads join or leave the motorway.

The studs between the left-hand lane and the hard shoulder are coloured red.

Question
In normal riding your position on the road should be

Mark one answer
- ● **about central in your lane**
- ○ about a foot from the kerb
- ○ on the right of your lane
- ○ near the centre of the road

If you are riding a motorcycle it is very important to ride where other road users can see you. In normal weather you should ride in the centre of your lane. This will

- help you to be seen in the mirror of the vehicle in front
- avoid uneven road surfaces in the gutter
- allow others to overtake on the right if they wish

Question
You are driving on a well-lit motorway at night. You must

Mark one answer
- ● **always use your headlights**
- ○ always use rear fog lights
- ○ use only your sidelights
- ○ use headlights only in bad weather

If you are driving on a motorway at night you must always use your headlights, even if the road is well lit.

Question

You are driving on a motorway at night.
You MUST have your headlights switched on
unless

Mark one answer

- ● **your vehicle is broken down on the hard shoulder**
- ○ there are vehicles close in front of you
- ○ you are travelling below 50 mph
- ○ the motorway is lit

Always use your headlights at night on a motorway unless you are stopped on the hard shoulder. If you break down and have to stop on the hard shoulder switch off the main beam. Leave the sidelights on so that other road users can see your vehicle or machine.

Question

You are travelling on a motorway at night with other vehicles just ahead of you.
Which lights should you have on?

Mark one answer

- ● **Dipped headlights**
- ○ Front fog lights
- ○ Main beam headlights
- ○ Sidelights only

If you are driving or riding behind other traffic at night on the motorway

- leave a two-second time gap
- dip your headlights

Full beam will dazzle the driver ahead. Your light beam should fall short of the vehicle in front.

Question

Which TWO of the following are correct?
When overtaking at night you should

Mark two answers

- ● **be careful because you can see less**
- ● **beware of bends in the road ahead**
- ○ wait until a bend so you can see the oncoming headlights
- ○ sound your horn twice before moving out
- ○ put headlights on full beam

Only overtake the vehicle in front if it is really necessary. At night the risks are increased due to the poor visibility. Don't overtake if there is a possibility of

- road junctions
- bends ahead
- the brow of a bridge or hill, except on a dual carriageway
- pedestrian crossings
- road markings indicating double white lines ahead
- vehicles changing direction
- any other potential hazard

Question

You are overtaking a car at night.
You must be sure that

Mark one answer

- ● **you do not dazzle other road users**
- ○ you flash your headlamps before overtaking
- ○ your rear fog lights are switched on
- ○ you have switched your lights to full beam before overtaking

If you wish to overtake at night ensure that your lights don't reflect in the mirror of the car in front. Wait until you have overtaken before switching to full beam.

Question
You are travelling at night.
You are dazzled by headlights coming towards you.
You should

Mark one answer
- ● slow down or stop
- ○ pull down your sun visor
- ○ switch on your main beam headlights
- ○ put your hand over your eyes

Question
You are dazzled by oncoming headlights when driving at night.
What should you do?

Mark one answer
- ● Slow down or stop
- ○ Brake hard
- ○ Drive faster past the oncoming car
- ○ Flash your lights

If you are driving at night there will be extra hazards to deal with. The lights of oncoming vehicles can often distract. If you are dazzled by them don't

- close your eyes
- flash your headlights. This will only distract the other driver too

Slow down or stop and let your eyes readjust.

Speeds and distances are more difficult to judge at night. You can't see as far as in daylight so less information is available. Don't take risks, especially if you are considering overtaking the vehicle in front.

Question
You are on a narrow road at night.
A slower-moving vehicle ahead has been signalling right for some time.
What should you do?

Mark one answer
- ● Wait for the signal to be cancelled before overtaking
- ○ Overtake on the left
- ○ Flash your headlights before overtaking
- ○ Signal right and sound your horn

If the vehicle in front has been indicating right for some time but has made no attempt to do so, wait for the signal to be cancelled. Don't

- flash your headlights
- sound your horn
- overtake without being able to see well down the road

Question
You intend to park on a road at night without lights.
Which of the following is right?

Mark one answer

● **The road must have a speed limit of 30 mph or less**

○ Your vehicle must be visible from at least 10 metres (33 feet)

○ You must park facing opposite the traffic flow

○ You must park at least half of your vehicle on the pavement

If you intend to park your vehicle park in the direction of the traffic. This will enable other road users to see the reflectors on the rear of your vehicle or machine. Use your sidelights if the speed limit is over 30 mph or your vehicle is over 1 tonne.

Question
You are driving along a major road with many side roads.
What precaution should you take?

Mark one answer

● **Slow down in case a vehicle pulls out**

○ Sound your horn as you reach each side road

○ Stop at each side road and check for traffic

○ Keep well out near the centre of the road

If you are driving or riding along a road where there are many side roads be alert. Look well ahead and anticipate the actions of other road users. Drive at a speed that will allow you to stop safely if a vehicle pulls out in front of you. The other driver might not see you if there are a lot of parked cars blocking the view.

Question
When riding along you should never

Mark one answer

● **look down at the front wheel**

○ brake using the front brake only

○ look over your left shoulder

○ ride with one hand off the handlebars

When you are manoeuvring your motorcycle the weight might make it awkward to handle. However when you are riding the weight improves the stability and balance. Never look down at the front wheel when riding because this can severely upset your balance. You should be looking at the road ahead and anticipating any hazards which may occur.

DSA THEORY TEST for cars and motorcycles

Question
Which TWO are correct?
The passing places on a single-track road are

Mark two answers

● to pull into if an oncoming vehicle wants to proceed

● to pull into if the car behind wants to overtake

○ for taking a rest from driving

○ for stopping and checking your route

○ to turn the car around in, if you are lost

If you are driving on a single-track road be prepared to pull over and let other road users pass. There are passing places to enable you to do this. These should not be used for parking or turning your car around.

Question
You see a vehicle coming towards you on a single-track road.
You should

Mark one answer

● stop at a passing place

○ reverse back to the main road

○ do an emergency stop

○ put on your hazard flashers

You must take extra care when driving on single-track roads. You may not be able to see around bends due to high hedges or fences. Drive with caution and expect to meet oncoming vehicles around the next bend. If you do, pull over into or opposite a passing place.

This section looks at motorway rules.

The questions will ask you about

- Speed limits
- Lane discipline
- Stopping
- Lighting
- Parking

Question

Which of the following CAN travel on a motorway?

Mark one answer

- Vans
- Cyclists
- Farm tractors
- Learner drivers

Question

Which FOUR of these must NOT use motorways?

Mark four answers

- Learner car drivers
- Farm tractors
- Horse riders
- Cyclists
- Motorcycles over 50cc
- Double-decker buses

Question

Which FOUR of these must NOT use motorways?

Mark four answers

- Learner car drivers
- Farm tractors
- Learner motorcyclists
- Cyclists
- Motorcycles over 50cc
- Double-decker buses

Question

A motorcycle is not allowed on a motorway if it has an engine size smaller than

Mark one answer

- 50cc
- 125cc
- 150cc
- 250cc

Motorways are designed to help traffic travel quickly. Traffic can only travel safely at high speed if the road is clear. Any slow-moving road user would be a danger to themselves and passing traffic. For this reason there are restrictions on who can use the motorway.

Motorways should NOT be used by

- pedestrians
- cyclists
- horse riders
- motorcycles under 50cc
- learner drivers
- certain slow-moving vehicles without permission
- invalid carriages not weighing more than 254kg (560 lbs)
- farm vehicles and animals

When you have passed your practical driving test it is a good idea to have some lessons on motorway driving. Statistically, motorways are safer than other roads, but they have rules that you need to know before you venture out for the first time.

PASS PLUS

NEW DRIVER GUIDE

Question

Why is it particularly important to carry out a check on your vehicle before making a long motorway journey?

Mark one answer

- **Continuous high speeds may increase the risk of your vehicle breaking down**
- You will have to do more harsh braking on motorways
- Motorway service stations do not deal with breakdowns
- The road surface will wear down the tyres faster

Question

You are joining a motorway from a slip road. You should

Mark one answer

- **match the speed of the traffic and move into a clear space**
- wait for a vehicle in the nearest lane to move over
- wait at the beginning of the slip road for the traffic to clear
- wait at the end of the slip road for a safe gap

Before you start your journey make sure your vehicle can cope with the demands of high-speed driving. Before starting a motorway journey check your vehicle's

- oil
- water
- tyres

Plan your rest stops if you are travelling a long way.

Join the motorway by using the slip road which leads to the acceleration lane. Adjust your speed to match the traffic already on the motorway. Indicate your intention to other road users, then move into a clear space. Don't

- force your way onto the motorway
- drive along the hard shoulder

Question
You are joining a motorway.
Why is it important to make full use of the slip road?

Mark one answer

● **To build up a speed similar to traffic on the motorway**

○ Because there is space available to slow down if you need to

○ To allow you direct access to the overtaking lanes

○ Because you can continue on the hard shoulder

Question
When joining a motorway you must

Mark one answer

● **always give way to traffic already on the motorway**

○ always use the hard shoulder

○ stop at the end of the acceleration lane

○ come to a stop before joining the motorway

Question
You are driving a car on a motorway.
Unless signs show otherwise you must NOT exceed

Mark one answer

● **70 mph**

○ 50 mph

○ 60 mph

○ 80 mph

Question
You are riding on a motorway.
Unless signs show otherwise you must NOT exceed

Mark one answer

● **70 mph**

○ 50 mph

○ 60 mph

○ 80 mph

The national speed limit for a car or a motorcycle on the motorway is 70 mph.

Lower speed limits may be in force so look out for the signs. There might be a variable speed limit in operation to control a very busy motorway. The speed limit may change depending on the volume of traffic. There may be roadworks enforcing a low speed limit.

Question

What is the national speed limit on motorways for cars and motorcycles?

Mark one answer

- ● **70 mph**
- ○ 30 mph
- ○ 50 mph
- ○ 60 mph

Speed limits may be altered due to weather conditions. Look out for signs on the central reserve or above your lane.

Question

You are towing a trailer on a motorway. What is your maximum speed limit?

Mark one answer

- ● **60 mph**
- ○ 40 mph
- ○ 50 mph
- ○ 70 mph

If you are towing a trailer on the motorway the speed limit is 60 mph. If you are towing a small, light trailer it will not reduce your vehicle's performance by very much.

Don't forget you are towing a trailer. Strong winds or buffeting from large vehicles might cause it to snake from side to side.

Question

On a three-lane motorway which lane should you use for normal driving?

Mark one answer

- ● **Left**
- ○ Right
- ○ Centre
- ○ Either the right or centre

On a three-lane motorway you should travel in the left-hand lane unless you are overtaking. This applies regardless of the speed you are travelling.

Question

A basic rule when driving on motorways is

Mark one answer

- ● **keep to the left lane unless overtaking**
- ○ use the lane that has least traffic
- ○ overtake on the side that is clearest
- ○ try to keep above 50 mph to prevent congestion

Question

You are driving on a three-lane motorway at 70 mph. There is no traffic ahead. Which lane should you use?

Mark one answer

- ● **Left lane**
- ○ Any lane
- ○ Middle lane
- ○ Right lane

DSA THEORY TEST for cars and motorcycles

Question
The left-hand lane on a three-lane motorway is for use by

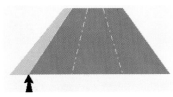

Mark one answer

● **any vehicle**
○ large vehicles only
○ emergency vehicles only
○ slow vehicles only

Question
The left-hand lane of a motorway should be used for

Mark one answer

● **normal driving**
○ breakdowns and emergencies only
○ overtaking slower traffic in the other lanes
○ slow vehicles only

On a motorway all traffic should use the left lane unless overtaking. If you need to overtake use the centre or right-hand lanes.

Make sure you move back to the left lane when you have finished overtaking. Don't stay in the middle or right-hand lanes if the left-hand lane is free.

You must be aware that large vehicles are not allowed into the right-hand lane to overtake. Don't impede their progress by staying in the middle lane. Move back into the left-hand lane as soon as it is safe to do so.

Question

For what reason may you use the right-hand lane of a motorway?

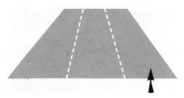

Mark one answer

- **For overtaking other vehicles**
- For keeping out of the way of lorries
- For driving at more than 70 mph
- For turning right

Question

On motorways you should never overtake on the left UNLESS

Mark one answer

- **there is a queue of traffic to your right that is moving more slowly**
- you can see well ahead that the hard shoulder is clear
- the traffic in the right-hand lane is signalling right
- you warn drivers behind by signalling left

Question

On a motorway you may ONLY stop on the hard shoulder

Mark one answer

- **in an emergency**
- if you feel tired and need to rest
- if you accidentally go past the exit that you wanted to take
- to pick up a hitchhiker

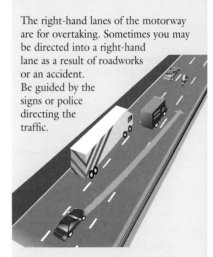

The right-hand lanes of the motorway are for overtaking. Sometimes you may be directed into a right-hand lane as a result of roadworks or an accident. Be guided by the signs or police directing the traffic.

Only overtake on the left if traffic is moving slowly in queues and the traffic on the right is moving slower.

Only use the hard shoulder in an emergency.

Don't stop on the hard shoulder to

- have a rest or a picnic
- pick up hitchhikers
- check a road map

Never reverse along the hard shoulder if you accidentally go past the exit you wanted.

Question
You get a puncture on the motorway.
You manage to get your vehicle onto the hard shoulder.
You should

Due to the danger from passing traffic you should not attempt repairs on the hard shoulder. Use the emergency telephone to call for assistance.

Mark one answer

- **use the emergency telephone and call for assistance**
- change the wheel yourself immediately
- try to wave down another vehicle for help
- only change the wheel if you have a passenger to help you

Question
What should you use the hard shoulder of a motorway for?

Mark one answer

- **Stopping in an emergency**
- Overtaking
- Stopping when you are tired
- Joining the motorway

Question
Your car has broken down on the motorway.
You have stopped on the hard shoulder.
Where is the safest place for you to wait for help?

If you do break down on the motorway stop on the hard shoulder.

Try to stop near an emergency phone. If this isn't possible follow the arrows on the marker posts. They will direct you to the nearest phone. Don't cross the motorway to reach a phone on the other side.

Mark one answer

- **On the grass bank**
- Behind the car
- In the car
- In front of the car

Question
You have broken down on a motorway.
Your vehicle is on the hard shoulder.
Your passengers should

Mark one answer
- ● **leave the vehicle and wait on the embankment**
- ○ stay in their seats with their seat belts on
- ○ leave the vehicle and walk to the nearest exit from the motorway
- ○ undo their seat belts but stay in their seats

Question
Your vehicle has broken down on a motorway.
You are not able to stop on the hard shoulder.
What should you do FIRST?

Mark one answer
- ● **Switch on your hazard warning lights**
- ○ Stop following traffic and ask for help
- ○ Attempt to repair your vehicle quickly
- ○ Place a warning triangle in the road

Question
You are travelling in the left-hand lane of a busy motorway.
Signs indicate that your lane is closed 800 yards ahead.
You should

Mark one answer
- ● **move over to the lane on your right as soon as it is safe**
- ○ signal right, then pull up and wait for someone to give way
- ○ switch on your hazard warning lights and edge over to the lane on your right
- ○ wait until you reach the obstruction, then move across to the right

The safest place to wait for assistance is on the grass bank away from the traffic. If you have passengers it is safer for them to leave the vehicle and wait on the embankment. Always leave the vehicle by the door away from the traffic. Keep children under control and well away from the carriageway.

If you can't reach the hard shoulder put on your hazard warning lights to warn others.

DON'T TRY TO REPAIR THE VEHICLE.

Always look well ahead and be aware of road signs. If you see that your lane will be closing move across to the next lane in good time. The road signs will have given plenty of warning. Don't

- wait until the last moment before trying to change lane
- expect someone to let you in
- stop

DSA THEORY TEST for cars and motorcycles

Question
When may you stop on a motorway?

Mark three answers

⬤ **If red lights show above the lanes**
⬤ **When told to by the police**
⬤ **In an emergency or a breakdown**
⬭ If you have to read a map
⬭ When you are tired and need a rest
⬭ If a child in the car feels ill

You may only stop on the carriageway of a motorway

• when told to do so by the police
• when flashing red lights show above the lane you are in
• in a traffic jam
• in an emergency or breakdown

Question
You are driving on a motorway.
There are red flashing lights above each lane.
You must

Flashing red lights above every lane mean you must not go on any further. You will also see a red cross illuminated. Stop and wait. Don't

• change lanes
• continue
• pull onto the hard shoulder (unless in an emergency)

Mark one answer

⬤ **stop and wait**
⬭ pull onto the hard shoulder
⬭ slow down and watch for further signals
⬭ leave at the next exit

Question
When driving through a contraflow system on a motorway you should

When driving through a contraflow system keep well back from the vehicle ahead. There is likely to be a speed restriction in force. Keep to this. Don't

• switch lanes
• drive too close to other traffic

Mark one answer

⬤ **keep a good distance from the vehicle ahead, for safety**
⬭ ensure that you do not exceed 30 mph, for safety
⬭ switch lanes to keep the traffic flowing
⬭ drive close to the vehicle ahead to reduce queues

Question

What do these motorway signs show?

Mark one answer

- ● **They are countdown markers to the next exit**
- ○ They are countdown markers to a bridge
- ○ They are distance markers to the next telephone
- ○ They warn of a police control ahead

Question

You are driving on a motorway.
By mistake, you go past the exit which you wanted to take.
You should

Mark one answer

- ● **carry on to the next exit**
- ○ carefully reverse on the hard shoulder
- ○ carefully reverse in the left-hand lane
- ○ make a U-turn at the next gap in the central reservation

Question

On a motorway the amber studs can be found between

Mark one answer

- ● **the central reservation and the carriageway**
- ○ the hard shoulder and the carriageway
- ○ the acceleration lane and the carriageway
- ○ each pair of the lanes

The exit from a motorway is indicated by countdown markers. These are positioned 100 metres (330 feet) apart, the first being 300 metres (990 feet) from the slip road. Try to get yourself into the left lane in good time.

If you miss an exit go on to the next one. Don't

- reverse anywhere
- make a U-turn

On motorways reflective studs are fitted into the road to help you

- in the dark
- in conditions of poor visibility

The reflective studs are coloured. These will help you to know which lane you are in and where slip roads join or leave the motorway.

DSA THEORY TEST for cars and motorcycles

Question
You are driving on a three-lane motorway. There are red reflective studs on your left and white ones to your right.
Where are you?

Mark one answer
- ● **In the left-hand lane**
- ○ In the right-hand lane
- ○ In the middle lane
- ○ On the hard shoulder

Question
What colour are the reflective studs between a motorway and its slip road?

Mark one answer
- ● **Green**
- ○ Amber
- ○ White
- ○ Red

Question
You are travelling on a motorway.
What colour are the reflective studs on the left of the carriageway?

Mark one answer
- ● **Red**
- ○ Green
- ○ White
- ○ Amber

The colours of the reflective studs on the motorway and their locations are

Red
- between the hard shoulder and the carriageway

White
- lane markings

Amber
- between the edge of the carriageway and the central reserve

Green
- along slip road exits and entrances

Bright Green/Yellow
- roadworks and contraflow systems

When you have passed your practical test ask your Approved Driving Instructor about lessons on the motorway. Good professional instruction will help you to become confident and safe on the motorway.

This section looks at rules of the road.

The questions will ask you about

- Speed limits
- Lane discipline
- Parking
- Lighting

Question

What is the national speed limit for cars and motorcycles on a dual carriageway?

Mark one answer

- 70 mph
- 30 mph
- 50 mph
- 60 mph

Question

You are driving along a road which has no traffic signs.
There are street lights.
What is the speed limit?

Mark one answer

- 30 mph
- 20 mph
- 40 mph
- 60 mph

Question

There are no speed limit signs on the road.
How is a 30 mph limit indicated?

Mark one answer

- By street lighting
- By hazard warning lines
- By pedestrian islands
- By double or single yellow lines

Question

Where you see street lights but no speed limit signs the limit is usually

Mark one answer

- 30 mph
- 40 mph
- 50 mph
- 60 mph

Ensure that you know the speed limit for the road you are driving on.

The speed limit on a dual carriageway or motorway is 70 mph for cars and motorcycles, unless there are signs to indicate otherwise.

The speed limits for different vehicles are listed in *The Highway Code*.

If you are not sure of the speed limit it can be indicated by the presence of street lights. If there is street lighting the speed limit will be 30 mph UNLESS otherwise indicated.

Question
You see this sign ahead of you.
It means

Mark one answer
- ● **do not exceed 30 mph after passing it**
- ○ start to slow down to 30 mph after passing it
- ○ you are leaving the 30 mph speed limit area
- ○ the minimum speed limit ahead is 30 mph

Question
If you see a 30 mph limit ahead this means

Mark one answer
- ● **you must not exceed this speed**
- ○ the restriction applies only during the working day
- ○ it is a guide. You are allowed to drive 10% faster
- ○ you must keep your speed up to 30 mph

Question
What does a speed limit sign like this mean?

Mark one answer
- ● **You must not exceed the speed shown**
- ○ It is safe to drive at the speed shown
- ○ The speed shown is the advised maximum
- ○ The speed shown allows for various road and weather conditions

If you are entering a lower speed limit adjust your speed in good time. Don't

- brake sharply
- wait until you are beyond the limit sign before slowing down

Because the sign is round it gives you an order. You must obey it.

In a built-up area there are many hazards which call for reduced speed, such as

- pedestrians
- cyclists
- junctions
- busy traffic situations

Speed limit signs are there for a reason. There may be a large number of side roads. The lower speed limit makes emerging from these safer.

Question
You are driving along a street with parked vehicles on the left-hand side.
For which THREE reasons must you keep your speed down?

Mark three answers

- ● **Vehicles may be pulling out**
- ● **Drivers' doors may open**
- ● **Children may run out from between the vehicles**
- ○ So that oncoming traffic can see you more clearly
- ○ You may set off car alarms

Question
You meet an obstruction on your side of the road. You must

Mark one answer

- ● **give way to oncoming traffic**
- ○ drive on, it is your right of way
- ○ wave oncoming vehicles through
- ○ accelerate to get past first

Question
You are leaving your vehicle parked on a road. When may you leave the engine running?

Mark one answer

- ● **Not on any occasion**
- ○ If you will be parked for less than five minutes
- ○ If the battery is flat
- ○ If there is a passenger in the vehicle

Care must be taken when in a built-up area where there are parked vehicles. Beware of

- vehicles pulling out, especially motorcycles which are small and difficult to see
- pedestrians, especially children who may run out from between cars
- drivers opening vehicle doors

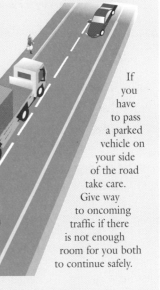

If you have to pass a parked vehicle on your side of the road take care. Give way to oncoming traffic if there is not enough room for you both to continue safely.

When you leave your vehicle parked on a road

- switch off the engine
- make sure there are no valuables visible
- shut all the windows
- lock the vehicle. Use an anti-theft device if you have one

Question

In which FOUR places must you NOT park or wait?

Mark four answers

- ⬤ **At a bus stop**
- ⬤ **Opposite a traffic island**
- ⬤ **In front of someone else's drive**
- ⬤ **On the brow of a hill**
- ⬭ On a dual carriageway
- ⬭ On the slope of a hill

Question

What is the nearest you may park your vehicle to a junction?

Mark one answer

- ⬤ **10 metres (33 feet)**
- ⬭ 12 metres (40 feet)
- ⬭ 15 metres (50 feet)
- ⬭ 20 metres (65 feet)

Question

In which TWO places must you NOT park?

Mark two answers ✓

- ⬤ **Near a school entrance**
- ⬤ **At a bus stop**
- ⬭ Near a police station
- ⬭ In a side road
- ⬭ In a one-way street

Care and thought should be taken when parking your own vehicle. Don't park

- on a footpath, pavement or cycle track
- near a school entrance
- at or near a bus stop
- on the approach to a zebra crossing
- within 10 metres (33 feet) of a junction (except in an authorised parking place)
- near a brow of a hill or humpback bridge
- opposite a traffic island or another parked vehicle
- where you would force other traffic to enter a tram lane
- where the kerb has been lowered to help wheelchair users
- in front of an entrance to a property
- where it might obstruct a tram

It may be tempting to park where you shouldn't while you run a quick errand. Careless parking could endanger other road users.

Question
At which of these places are you **sometimes** allowed to park your vehicle?

Mark one answer

- **Where there is a single broken yellow line**
- On the nearside lane of a motorway
- On a clearway
- On the zigzag lines of a zebra crossing

Question
What MUST you have to park in a disabled space?

Mark one answer

- **An orange badge**
- A wheelchair
- An advanced driver certificate
- A modified vehicle

Question
Your vehicle is parked on the road at night. When must you use sidelights?

Mark one answer

- **Where the speed limit exceeds 30 mph**
- Where there are continuous white lines in the middle of the road
- Where you are facing oncoming traffic
- Where you are near a bus stop

You may be able to park where there are broken lines along the edge of the road. Check the road signs at the side of the road for parking restrictions. Where there are double yellow lines you may not be able to park there at all.

Don't park in a space reserved for disabled people unless you or your passenger are a disabled badge-holder. The badge must be displayed on your vehicle in the bottom left-hand corner of the windscreen.

When parking at night park in the direction of the traffic. This will enable other road users to see the reflectors on the rear of your vehicle.

Use your sidelights if the speed limit is over 30 mph or you are parking a vehicle over 1,525 kg.

Question
On a three-lane dual carriageway the right-hand lane can be used for

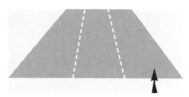

Mark one answer
- ● **overtaking or turning right**
- ○ overtaking only, never turning right
- ○ fast-moving traffic only
- ○ turning right only, never overtaking

Question
You are driving on a two-lane dual carriageway. For which TWO of these would you use the right-hand lane?

Mark two answers
- ● **Turning right**
- ● **Overtaking slower traffic**
- ○ Normal driving
- ○ Driving at the minimum allowed speed
- ○ Constant high-speed driving
- ○ Mending punctures

Question
You are driving in the right lane of a dual carriageway.
You see signs showing that the right lane is closed 800 yards ahead.
You should

Mark one answer
- ● **move to the left in good time**
- ○ keep in that lane until you reach the queue
- ○ move to the left immediately
- ○ wait and see which lane is moving faster

When on a dual carriageway use the left-hand lane. Only use the right-hand lane for

- overtaking
- turning right

When overtaking on a dual carriageway be on the lookout for vehicles ahead which are turning right. They are likely to be slowing or stopped. You need to see them in good time so that you can take appropriate action.

If you overtake on a dual carriageway move back into the left lane as soon as it is safe. Don't cut in across the path of the vehicle you have just passed.

Keep a lookout for traffic signs. If you are directed to change lanes, do so in good time. Don't

- push your way into traffic in another lane
- leave changing lanes until the last moment

Question
As a car driver which THREE lanes must you NOT use?

Mark three answers
- ● **Bus lane at the times shown**
- ● **Cycle lane**
- ● **Tram lane**
- ○ Crawler lane
- ○ Overtaking lane
- ○ Acceleration lane

Look out for signs or road markings that tell you which lane to use. Some lanes can only be used by certain road users. Don't use

- bus lanes at the times shown
- cycle lanes
- tram lanes

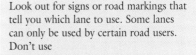

Question
As a motorcycle rider which TWO lanes must you NOT use?

Mark two answers
- ● **Cycle lane**
- ● **Tram lane**
- ○ Crawler lane
- ○ Overtaking lane
- ○ Acceleration lane

In some towns motorcycles are permitted to use bus lanes. Check the signs carefully.

Question
Where may you overtake on a one-way street?

Mark one answer
- ● **Either on the right or the left**
- ○ Only on the left-hand side
- ○ Overtaking is not allowed
- ○ Only on the right-hand side

You can overtake other traffic on either side when travelling in a one-way street. Look for signs and road markings and use the most suitable lane for your destination.

Question
You are going along a single-track road with passing places only on the right.
The driver behind wishes to overtake.
You should

Mark one answer
- ● **wait opposite a passing place on your right**
- ○ speed up to get away from the following driver
- ○ switch on your hazard warning lights
- ○ drive into a passing place on your right

Some roads are only wide enough for one vehicle. Often this type of road has special passing places where the road is widened for a short distance.

If there is a car coming toward you, pull into a passing place on your left or stop opposite one on your right. Don't

- force other vehicles to reverse
- pull into the passing place on the right

Question

You are on a road which is only wide enough for one vehicle. There is a car coming towards you. Which TWO of these would be correct?

Mark two answers

- ● **Pull into a passing place on your left**
- ● **Wait opposite a passing place on your right**
- ○ Pull into a passing place on your right
- ○ Force the other driver to reverse
- ○ Pull into a passing place if your vehicle is wider
- ○ Wait opposite a passing place on your left

If you meet another vehicle in a narrow road and the passing place is on the right, pull up opposite it. This will allow the oncoming vehicle to pull into it and pass you safely.

Question

When going straight ahead at a roundabout you should

Mark one answer

- ● **indicate before leaving the roundabout**
- ○ not indicate at any time
- ○ indicate right when approaching the roundabout
- ○ indicate left when approaching the roundabout

When you want to go ahead at a roundabout indicate left just after you pass the exit before the one you wish to take. Don't

- signal right on approach
- signal left on approach

Question

You are going straight ahead at a roundabout. How should you signal?

Mark one answer

- ● **Signal left just after you pass the exit before the one you will take**
- ○ Signal right on the approach and then left to leave the roundabout
- ○ Signal left as you leave the exit off the roundabout
- ○ Signal left on the approach to the roundabout and keep the signal on until you leave

To go straight ahead at a roundabout you should normally approach in the left-hand lane. Where there are road markings use the lane indicated.

Ensure that you signal correctly and in good time. Other road users need to know your intentions.

Question
At a crossroads there are no signs or road markings.
Two vehicles approach.
Which has priority?

Mark one answer
- ● **Neither vehicle**
- ○ The vehicle travelling the fastest
- ○ The vehicle on the widest road
- ○ Vehicles approaching from the right

At a crossroads where there are no 'give way' signs or road markings BE VERY CAREFUL. No vehicle has priority, even if the size of the roads are different.

Question
Who has priority at an unmarked crossroads?

Mark one answer
- ● **No one**
- ○ The driver of the larger vehicle
- ○ The driver who is going faster
- ○ The driver on the wider road

Practise good observation in all directions before you emerge or make a turn.

Question
You are intending to turn right at a junction.
An oncoming driver is also turning right.
It will normally be safer to

Mark one answer
- ● **keep the other vehicle to your RIGHT and turn behind it (offside to offside)**
- ○ keep the other vehicle to your LEFT and turn in front of it (nearside to nearside)
- ○ carry on and turn at the next junction instead
- ○ hold back and wait for the other driver to turn first

When turning right at a junction if the oncoming vehicle is also turning right keep the other vehicle to your right and pass offside to offside.

At some junctions the layout may make it difficult to turn this way. Be prepared to pass nearside to nearside, but take extra care. Your view ahead will be obscured by the vehicle turning in front of you.

Question
When may you enter a box junction?

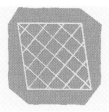

Mark one answer
- ● **Only when your exit road is clear**
- ○ Only when there are less than two vehicles in front of you
- ○ Whenever the traffic lights show green
- ○ Whenever you need to turn right

Box junctions are marked on the road to prevent the road becoming blocked.

DON'T enter the box unless your exit road is clear. You may only wait in the box if your exit road is clear but oncoming traffic is preventing you from completing the turn.

Question
On which THREE occasions MUST you stop your vehicle?

Mark three answers
- ● **When involved in an accident**
- ● **At a red traffic light**
- ● **When signalled to do so by a police officer**
- ○ At a junction with double broken white lines
- ○ At a pelican crossing when the amber light is flashing and no pedestrians are crossing

Don't stop or hold up traffic unnecessarily. However you MUST stop when signalled to do so by

- a police officer
- a school crossing patrol
- a red traffic light

or when you have had an accident

Question
You MUST stop when signalled to do so by which THREE of these?

Mark three answers
- ● **A police officer**
- ● **A school crossing patrol**
- ● **A red traffic light**
- ○ A pedestrian
- ○ A bus driver

Looking well ahead and 'reading' the road will help you to anticipate hazards. This will allow you to stop safely if asked to do so by a person or a road sign.

DSA THEORY TEST for cars and motorcycles

Question
You are waiting at a level crossing.
The red warning lights continue to flash after a train has passed by.
What should you do?

At a level crossing flashing red lights mean you should stop.

On some crossings you will also hear an alarm bell. If the train passes but the lights keep flashing and the alarm continues to sound, wait. There may be another train coming.

Mark one answer

● **Continue to wait**
○ Get out and investigate
○ Telephone the signal operator
○ Drive across carefully

Question
You are driving over a level crossing.
The warning lights come on and a bell rings.
What should you do?

If you are already on the crossing when the lights come on, keep going. Don't stop on the crossing.

If the warning lights come on as you are approaching the crossing, stop. Don't try to dart across before the train comes.

Mark one answer

● **Keep going and clear the crossing**
○ Get everyone out of the vehicle immediately
○ Stop and reverse back to clear the crossing
○ Stop immediately and use your hazard warning lights

Question
You are waiting at a level crossing.
A train has passed but the lights keep flashing.
You must

Mark one answer

● **carry on waiting**
○ phone the signal operator
○ edge over the stop line and look for trains
○ park your vehicle and investigate

If the lights at a level crossing continue to flash after a train has passed continue to wait as there might be another train coming. Time seems to pass slowly when you are held up in a queue. Be patient and wait until the lights stop flashing.

Question
At a pelican crossing what does a flashing amber light mean?

Mark one answer

● **You must give way to pedestrians still on the crossing**
○ You must not move off until the lights stop flashing
○ You can move off, even if pedestrians are still on the crossing
○ You must stop because the lights are about to change to red

A flashing amber light at a pelican crossing means that you must give way to people on the crossing. If the road is clear then proceed. The green light will show after the flashing amber.

Question
You are on a busy main road and find you are travelling in the wrong direction.
What should you do?

Mark one answer

● **Turn round in a side road**
○ Turn into a side road on the right and reverse into the main road
○ Make a U-turn in the main road
○ Make a 'three-point' turn in the main road

If want to turn your car around don't

• turn in a busy street
• reverse into a main road

Find a quiet side road. Choose a place where you will not obstruct an entrance or exit, and look out for pedestrians and cyclists as well as other traffic.

Question
You are parked in a busy high street.
What is the safest way to turn your vehicle around to go the opposite way?

Mark one answer

● **Find a quiet side road to turn round in**
○ Drive into a side road and reverse into the main road
○ Get someone to stop the traffic
○ Do a U-turn

If you ride a motorcycle don't make a U-turn in a busy road.

DSA THEORY TEST **for cars and motorcycles**

Question
You MUST NOT reverse

Mark one answer
- ● **for longer than necessary**
- ○ for more than a car's length
- ○ into a side road
- ○ in a built-up area

Question
When may you reverse from a side road into a main road?

Mark one answer
- ● **NOT at any time**
- ○ Only if both roads are clear of traffic
- ○ At any time
- ○ Only if the main road is clear of traffic

You may decide to turn your vehicle around by reversing into an opening or side road. When you reverse always look behind and watch for pedestrians. Don't

- reverse for longer than is necessary
- reverse from a side road into a main road

Don't reverse into a main road from a side road. The main road is likely to be busy and the traffic on it moving quickly. Cut down the risks by using a quiet side road to reverse into.

This section looks at road and traffic signs.

The questions will ask you about

- Road signs
- Speed limits
- Road markings
- Regulations

Question
You MUST obey signs giving orders. These signs are mostly in

Traffic signs can be divided into three classes – those giving orders, those warning and those informing. On the road each class of sign has a different shape.

Mark one answer

● **red circles**
○ green rectangles
○ red triangles
○ blue rectangles

Question
Traffic signs giving orders are generally which shape?

Mark one answer

Road signs in the shape of a circle give orders. Those with a red circle are mostly prohibitive. The stop sign is octagonal to give it greater prominence. These signs must always be obeyed.

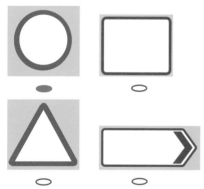

Question
Which type of sign tells you NOT to do something?

Mark one answer

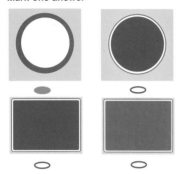

Question
Which sign means no vehicles are allowed?

Mark one answer

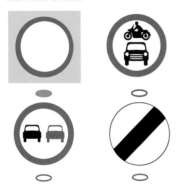

Signs in the shape of a circle mean that you are not allowed to do something. Study *Know Your Traffic Signs* to ensure that you understand the order you are shown.

Question
What does this sign mean?

Traffic may be prohibited from certain roads. A sign will indicate which types of vehicles are not allowed to use it. Make sure you know which signs apply to the vehicle you are using.

Mark one answer
- ● **No motor vehicles**
- ○ No overtaking
- ○ Clearway (no stopping)
- ○ Cars and motorcycles only

Question
Which sign means NO motor vehicles allowed?

Mark one answer ✓

Question
What does this sign mean?

The 'no overtaking' sign is in the shape of a circle so you must comply with this order. You may see it where there is a series of bends or the road is narrow.

Mark one answer
- ● **Do not overtake**
- ○ Oncoming cars have priority
- ○ Two-way traffic
- ○ No right turn ahead

Question
What does this sign mean?

Mark one answer
- ⬤ **No overtaking**
- ⬭ You have priority
- ⬭ No motor vehicles
- ⬭ Two-way traffic

Question
What does this sign mean?

Mark one answer
- ⬤ **Do not overtake**
- ⬭ Keep in one lane
- ⬭ Priority to traffic coming toward you
- ⬭ Form two lanes

Question
Which sign means no overtaking?

Mark one answer

⬭

⬭   ⬭

Road signs which show no overtaking will be placed in locations where passing the vehicle in front is dangerous. If you see this sign do not attempt to overtake. The sign is there for a reason and you must obey it.

If you are behind a slow-moving vehicle, be patient. Wait until the restriction no longer applies and you can overtake safely.

Question
What does this sign mean?

This sign indicates where waiting restrictions apply. There will be a plate or additional sign to tell you when the restrictions apply.

Mark one answer

- ● **Waiting restrictions apply**
- ○ Waiting permitted
- ○ National speed limit applies
- ○ Clearway (no stopping)

Question
You see this sign ahead.
It means

There are stretches of road where you are not allowed to stop (unless in an emergency). These are called 'clearways'. You will see this sign. Stopping where these restrictions apply may be dangerous and could cause an obstruction. Restrictions might apply for several miles and this may be indicated on the sign.

Mark one answer

- ● **no stopping**
- ○ national speed limit applies
- ○ waiting restrictions apply
- ○ no entry

Question
What does this traffic sign mean?

Priority signs are normally shown where the road is narrow and there is not enough room for two vehicles to pass, such as

- a narrow bridge
- at road works
- a width restriction

Make sure you know who has priority. Comply with the sign and don't force a right of way. Show courtesy and consideration to other road users.

Mark one answer

- ● **Give priority to oncoming traffic**
- ○ No overtaking allowed
- ○ No U-turns allowed
- ○ One-way traffic only

Question
What is the meaning of this traffic sign?

Mark one answer

- ● **You have priority over vehicles coming toward you**
- ○ End of two-way road
- ○ Give priority to vehicles coming toward you
- ○ Bus lane ahead

This sign shows that you have priority over the vehicles approaching. DONT FORCE A RIGHT OF WAY. Show courtesy and consideration to other road users.

Question
What does this sign mean?

Mark one answer

- ● **You have priority over vehicles from the opposite direction**
- ○ No overtaking
- ○ You are entering a one-way street
- ○ Two-way traffic ahead

Question
What should you do when you see this sign?

Mark one answer

- ● **Stop, even if the road is clear**
- ○ Stop, ONLY if traffic is approaching
- ○ Stop, ONLY if children are waiting to cross
- ○ Stop, ONLY if a red light is showing

A stop sign is shown on an octagonal shaped background. The sign will be at a junction where visibility is restricted or there is heavy traffic.

IT MUST BE OBEYED. YOU MUST STOP.

Practise good all-round observation before moving off.

Question
What does this sign mean?

Mark one answer
- ● **Minimum speed 30 mph**
- ○ Service area 30 miles ahead
- ○ Maximum speed 30 mph
- ○ Lay-by 30 miles ahead

Question
What does a circular traffic sign with a blue background do?

Mark one answer
- ● **Give an instruction**
- ○ Give warning of a motorway ahead
- ○ Give directions
- ○ Give motorway information

Question
What does a sign with a brown background show?

Mark one answer
- ● **Tourist directions**
- ○ Primary roads
- ○ Motorway routes
- ○ Minor routes

Signs with blue circles give a positive instruction. They will often be seen in towns or urban areas. For example

mini-roundabout

pass either side

Signs with a brown background give directions to places of interest. They will often be seen on the motorway directing you along the easiest route.

Question
What are triangular signs for?

Mark one answer

● **To give warnings**
○ To give information
○ To give orders
○ To give directions

Question
Which FOUR of these would be indicated by a triangular road sign?

Mark four answers

● **Road narrows**
● **Low bridge**
● **Children crossing**
● **T-junction**
○ Ahead only
○ Minimum speed

Question
What does this sign mean?

Mark one answer

● **You are approaching a cycle route**
○ Cyclists must dismount
○ Bicycles are not allowed
○ Walking is not allowed

Triangular signs are warning signs. They will tell you about the road ahead and what to expect. Get into the habit of checking each sign that you pass. This will warn you of the hazards ahead.

Where there is a cycle route a sign will show a bicycle in a red warning triangle. Watch out for children on bicycles and cyclists rejoining the main road.

DSA THEORY TEST for cars and motorcycles

Question
What does this sign mean?

Mark one answer

- ● **Pedestrian crossing ahead**
- ○ No footpath ahead
- ○ Pedestrians only ahead
- ○ School crossing ahead

Question
What does this sign mean?

Mark one answer

- ● **Pedestrian crossing ahead**
- ○ School crossing patrol
- ○ No pedestrians allowed
- ○ Pedestrian zone - no vehicles

Question
Which of these signs means there is a series of bends ahead?

Mark one answer

There are many signs relating to pedestrians. Study *The Highway Code* and *Know Your Traffic Signs*. Some of the signs look similar but give different warnings.

Triangular signs give you a warning of hazards ahead. They are there to give you time to adjust your speed and drive accordingly.

Question
What does this sign mean?

This sign may be at the end of a dual carriageway or a one-way street. The sign is there to warn you of oncoming traffic.

Mark one answer

⬤ **Two-way traffic straight ahead**
◯ Two-way traffic ahead across a one-way street
◯ Traffic approaching you has priority
◯ Motorway contraflow system ahead

Question
What does this sign mean?

Where weather conditions are often bad, signs will give you a warning. A sign with a picture of a wind-sock will indicate there may be strong crosswinds. This sign is often found on exposed roads.

Mark one answer

⬤ **Crosswinds**
◯ Road noise
◯ Airport
◯ Adverse camber

Question
What does this traffic sign mean?

A sign showing an exclamation mark (!) will alert you to the likelihood of danger ahead. Be ready for any situation that requires you to reduce your speed.

Mark one answer

⬤ **Danger ahead**
◯ Slippery road ahead
◯ Tyres liable to punctures ahead
◯ Service area ahead

Question
What does this sign mean?

Mark one answer
- ● **Ring road**
- ○ Route for lorries
- ○ Rest area
- ○ Roundabout

Question
What does this sign mean?

Mark one answer
- ● **Ring road**
- ○ Railway station
- ○ Route for cyclists
- ○ Scenic route

Question
What does this sign mean?

Mark one answer
- ● **The right-hand lane is closed**
- ○ The right-hand lane ahead is narrow
- ○ Right-hand lane for buses only
- ○ No turning to the right

Signs are also designed to give you advice. Ring road signs direct traffic around major towns and cities. Ring roads help the traffic to flow and ease congestion in town centres.

Temporary signs may tell you about roadworks or lane restrictions. Look well ahead. If you have to change lanes do so in good time.

Question

You see this traffic light ahead.
Which light(s) will come on next?

- ⬤ **Red alone**
- ⬯ Red and amber together
- ⬯ Green and amber together
- ⬯ Green alone

Question

You are approaching a red traffic light.
The signal will change from red to

- ⬤ **red and amber, then green**
- ⬯ green, then amber
- ⬯ amber, then green
- ⬯ green and amber, then green

At junctions controlled by traffic lights you must stop behind the white line until the lights change to green. Don't

- move forward when the red and amber lights are showing together
- proceed when the light is green if your exit road is blocked

If you are approaching traffic lights which are visible from a distance and the light has been green for some time it is likely to change. Try to anticipate this. Be ready to slow down and stop.

If you know which light is going to show next you can plan your approach accordingly. This will prevent excessive braking or hesitation at the junction.

Question
A red traffic light means

Mark one answer
- **you must stop and wait behind the stop line**
- you should stop unless turning left
- stop if you are able to brake safely
- proceed with caution

Question
At traffic lights, amber on its own means

Mark one answer
- **stop at the stop line**
- prepare to go
- go if the way is clear
- go if no pedestrians are crossing

Learn the sequence of traffic lights.

RED means stop and wait behind the stop line.

RED and AMBER also means stop. Don't go until the green light shows.

GREEN means you may go if your way is clear. Don't proceed if your exit road is blocked, and don't block the junction. Look out for pedestrians.

AMBER means stop at the stop line. You may go if the amber light appears after you have crossed the stop line or you are so close to it that to pull up might cause an accident.

Question
A red traffic light means

Mark one answer

- **you must stop behind the white stop line**
- you may drive straight on if there is no other traffic
- you may turn left if it is safe to do so
- you must slow down and prepare to stop if traffic has started to cross

Question
You are approaching traffic lights.
Red and amber are showing.
This means

Mark one answer

- **wait for the green light before you pass the lights**
- pass the lights if the road is clear
- there is a fault with the lights – take care
- the lights are about to change to red

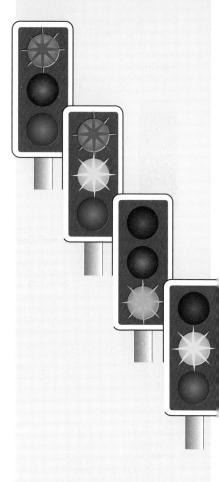

DSA **THEORY TEST** **for cars and motorcycles**

Question
You are at a junction controlled by traffic lights. When should you NOT proceed at green?

Mark one answer

● **When your exit from the junction is blocked**
○ When pedestrians are waiting to cross
○ When you think the lights may be about to change
○ When you intend to turn right

As you approach the lights look into the road you wish to take. Only proceed if your exit road is clear. If the road is blocked hold back, even if you have to wait for the next green signal.

Question
You are in the left-hand lane at traffic lights. You are waiting to turn left.
At which of these traffic lights must you NOT move on?

Mark one answer

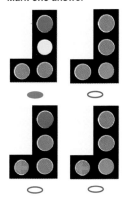

At some junction there may be a separate signal for each lane. These are called 'filter' lights. They are designed to help traffic flow at major junctions. Make sure you are in the correct lane and proceed if the green light shows.

Question
What does this sign mean?

Mark one answer

- ⬤ **Traffic lights out of order**
- ⬭ Amber signal out of order
- ⬭ Temporary traffic lights ahead
- ⬭ New traffic lights ahead

Where traffic lights are out of order you might see this sign. Proceed with caution as the the priority at the junction may not be clear.

Question
A pelican crossing shows the flashing green man signal.
What signal do drivers see?

Mark one answer

- ⬤ **Flashing amber**
- ⬭ Red and amber
- ⬭ Red
- ⬭ Flashing green

Pelican crossings are controlled crossings where pedestrians use push-button controls to change the signals.

If you are approaching and the amber light is flashing, be cautious. There may be pedestrians crossing the road. Give way to them.

Question
What do these zigzag lines at pedestrian crossings mean?

Mark one answer

- ⬤ **No parking at any time**
- ⬭ Parking allowed only for a short time
- ⬭ Slow down to 20 mph
- ⬭ Sounding horns is not allowed

The approach to hazards may be marked with signs on the road surface. The approach to a pedestrian crossing is marked with zigzag lines. Don't

- park on them
- overtake the leading vehicle when approaching the crossing

Parking here will block the view for pedestrians and the approaching traffic.

DSA THEORY TEST for cars and motorcycles

Question
These markings mean you are approaching

Mark one answer
- 🔴 **a pedestrian crossing**
- ⬭ a bus stop
- ⬭ a box junction
- ⬭ a parking zone

Question
A white line like this along the centre of the road is a

Mark one answer
- 🔴 **hazard warning**
- ⬭ bus lane marking
- ⬭ 'give way' marking
- ⬭ lane marking

Question
What does this road marking mean?

Mark one answer
- 🔴 **You are approaching a hazard**
- ⬭ Do not cross the line
- ⬭ No stopping allowed
- ⬭ No overtaking allowed

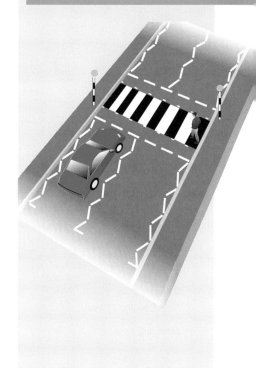

Road markings will warn you of a hazard ahead. A single broken line, with long markings and short gaps, along the centre of the road is a hazard warning line. Don't cross it unless you can see that the road is clear WELL ahead.

Question

Which is a hazard warning line?

Mark one answer

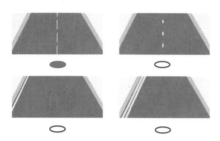

Look out for places where the single broken line on the road surface gets longer. This will mean there is a hazard ahead.

Question

At this junction there is a stop sign with a solid white line on the road surface.
Why is there a stop sign here?

Mark one answer

⬤ **Visibility along the major road is restricted**
◯ Speed on the major road is de-restricted
◯ It is a busy junction
◯ There are hazard warning lines in the centre of the road

If your view is restricted at a road junction you must stop. There may also be a stop sign. Don't emerge until you are sure there is no traffic approaching.

IF YOU DON'T KNOW, DON'T GO.

Question

You see this line across the road at a roundabout.
What does it mean?

Mark one answer

⬤ **Give way to traffic from the right**
◯ Traffic from the left has right of way
◯ You have right of way
◯ Stop at the line

A broken line across the entrance to a roundabout means give way to the right. Stay behind it until it is clear to emerge onto the roundabout.

DSA THEORY TEST for cars and motorcycles

Question

How will a police officer in a patrol vehicle get you to stop?

Mark one answer

- ● **Flash the headlights, indicate left and point to the left**
- ○ Wait until you stop, then approach you
- ○ Use the siren, overtake, cut in front and stop
- ○ Pull alongside you, use the siren and wave you to stop

You must obey signals given by the police. If a police officer in a patrol vehicle wants you to stop he or she will

- flash their headlights
- indicate left
- point to the left

They will do this without causing danger to you or other traffic. You must pull up on the left as soon as it is safe to do so and switch off your engine.

Question

There is a police car following you.
The police officer flashes the headlights and points to the left
What should you do?

Mark one answer

- ● **Pull up on the left**
- ○ Turn next left
- ○ Stop immediately
- ○ Move over to the left

Question

You approach a junction.
The traffic lights are not working.
A police officer gives this signal.
You should

If a police officer or traffic wardens are directing traffic you must obey them. They will use the arm signals shown in *The Highway Code*. Learn what these mean and act accordingly.

Mark one answer

- ● **stop at the stop line**
- ○ turn left only
- ○ turn right only
- ○ stop level with the officer's arm

Question
Which THREE are **legally** authorised to direct traffic?

Mark three answers

- A traffic warden
- A road worker operating a stop-go board
- A school crossing warden
- A farm worker in charge of livestock crossing the road
- A teacher in charge of children who are crossing the road
- Anyone assisting the driver of a large vehicle to reverse

You MUST obey a direction given by a

- police officer
- traffic warden
- school crossing patroller
- road worker with a stop-go board

DSA THEORY TEST for cars and motorcycles

Question
Which arm signal tells a following vehicle you intend to turn left?

Mark one answer

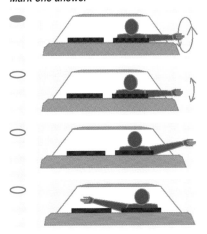

Question
How should you give an arm signal to turn left?

Mark one answer

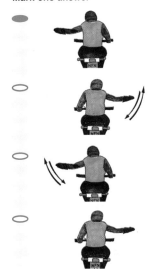

Timing of signals may depend on the layout of a junction. Don't signal too early, where you might mislead other road users.

There may be occasions when you need to give an arm signal. For example

- where other road users can't see your indicators
- in bright sunshine when your indicator may be difficult to see
- to reinforce a signal at a complex road layout

Make sure they are clear, correct and decisive.

Question
You are giving an arm signal ready to turn left. Why should you NOT continue with the arm signal while you turn?

Mark one answer

● **Because you will have less steering control**
○ Because you might hit a pedestrian on the corner
○ Because you will need to keep the clutch applied
○ Because other motorists will think you are stopping on the corner

Don't maintain an arm signal when turning. You should have full control of your machine at all times.

Question
You want to turn right at a junction but you think that your indicators cannot be seen clearly. What should you do?

Mark one answer

● **Give an arm signal as well as an indicator signal**
○ Get out and check if your indicators can be seen
○ Stay in the left-hand lane
○ Keep well over to the right

If you think your indicators can't be seen clearly give an approved arm signal.

Question
When may you sound the horn on your vehicle?

Mark one answer

● **To warn other drivers of your presence**
○ To give you right of way
○ To attract a friend's attention
○ To make slower drivers move over

Only use the horn to warn other road users of your presence. Don't use it aggressively. You must not sound the horn

• between 11.30 pm and 7 am
• when your vehicle is stationary, unless a moving vehicle poses a danger

Question
When motorists flash their headlights at you it means

Mark one answer   ✓

● **they are warning you of their presence**
○ there is a radar speed trap ahead
○ they are giving way to you
○ there is something wrong with your vehicle

If other drivers flash their headlights this is not a signal to show priority. The flashing of headlights has the same meaning as sounding the horn – it is a warning of their presence.

Question
You are waiting at a T-junction.
A vehicle is coming from the right with the left
signal flashing.
What should you do?

Mark one answer

● **Wait until the vehicle starts to turn in**
○ Move out and accelerate hard
○ Pull out before the vehicle reaches the
junction
○ Move out slowly

Question
When may you NOT overtake on the left?

Mark one answer

● **On a free-flowing motorway or dual
carriageway**
○ When the traffic is moving slowly in queues
○ On a one-way street
○ When the car in front is signalling to turn
right

Question
What does this motorway sign mean?

Mark one answer

● **Change to the lane on your left**
○ Leave the motorway at the next exit
○ Change to the opposite carriageway
○ Pull up on the hard shoulder

Try to anticipate the actions of other road
users. Their signals might be misleading.

When you are waiting at a junction don't
emerge if you will impede the progress of
other traffic. This can call for accurate
judgement.

You may only overtake on the left

• when traffic is moving slowly in queues
• when a vehicle ahead is positioned
to turn right and there is room to
pass on the left
• in a one-way street

Don't overtake on the left if the traffic on
a dual carriageway is flowing freely. Other
road users will not anticipate your action.

On the motorway, signs might show
temporary warnings. This allows for
different traffic or weather conditions
and might indicate

• lane closures
• speed limits
• weather warnings

Question
What does this motorway sign mean?

Mark one answer

- **Temporary maximum speed 50 mph**
- Temporary minimum speed 50 mph
- No services for 50 miles
- Obstruction 50 metres (165 feet) ahead

Look out for signs above your lane or on the central reserve. These will give you important information or warnings about the road ahead.

Due to the high speeds of motorway traffic these signs may light up some distance from any hazard. Don't ignore the signs just because the road looks clear to you.

Question
What does this sign mean?

Mark one answer

- **Right-hand lane closed ahead**
- Through traffic use left lane
- Right-hand lane T-junction only
- 11 tonne weight limit

Move over as soon as you see the sign and it is safe to do so. Don't stay in the lane, which is closed ahead, until the last moment to beat a queue of traffic.

Question
On a motorway this sign means

Mark one answer

- **move to the lane on your left**
- move over onto the hard shoulder
- pass a temporary obstruction on the left
- leave the motorway at the next exit

If signs instruct you to change lanes do so in good time.

DSA THEORY TEST for cars and motorcycles

Question
You are driving on a motorway.
Red flashing lights appear above your lane.
What should you do?

Mark one answer

● **Go no further in that lane**
○ Continue in that lane and await further information
○ Drive onto the hard shoulder
○ Stop and wait for an instruction to proceed

If flashing red lights appear above EVERY lane STOP, even if others don't.

Question
Where can you find amber studs on a motorway?

Mark one answer

● **On the right-hand edge of the road**
○ Separating the slip road from the motorway
○ On the left-hand edge of the road
○ Separating the lanes

At night or in poor visibility reflective studs in the road will help you to judge your position on the carriageway. Studs which are the colour green will also show you entry and exit lanes.

Question
Where on a motorway would you find green reflective studs?

Mark one answer

● **At slip road entrances and exits**
○ Separating driving lanes
○ Between the hard shoulder and the carriageway
○ Between the carriageway and the central reservation

Question
What does this sign mean?

When you leave the motorway make sure you check your speedometer. You may be going faster than you realise. Slow down using the slip road. Look out for speed limit signs.

Mark one answer

● **End of motorway**
○ No motor vehicles
○ No through road
○ End of bus lane

SECTION 12   DOCUMENTS

This section looks at the documents needed
for drivers and their vehicles.

The questions will ask you about

- Licences

- Insurance

- MOT test certificates

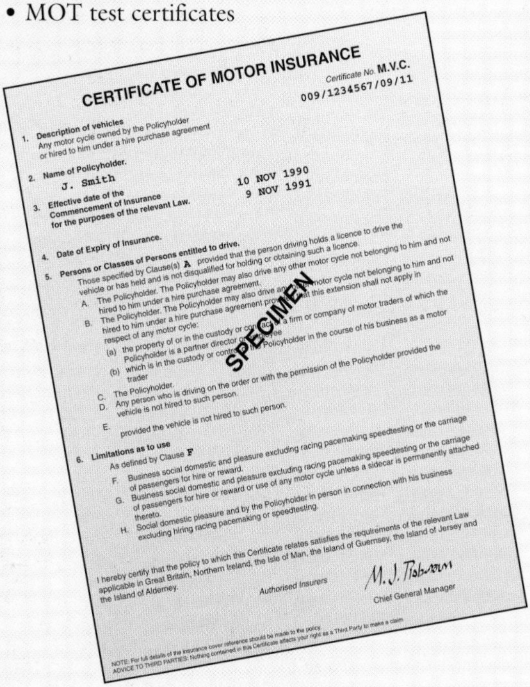

Question
To drive on the road learners MUST

Mark one answer

● **have a signed, valid provisional licence**
⬭ have NO penalty points on their licence
⬭ have taken professional instruction
⬭ apply for a driving test within 12 months

Before you drive on the road you must have a signed provisional licence. As soon as you have received your licence, sign it. It is not valid until you have done so.

Question
Until you pass your full motorcycle test you must

Mark one answer

● **display red 'L' plates on your bike**
⬭ display green 'L' plates on your bike
⬭ only ride when a qualified instructor is present
⬭ only ride when someone with a full licence is present

Until you have passed your full motorcycle test you must display red 'L' plates on your motorcycle. If you ride in Wales you can display a red 'D' plate. This stands for Dysgwr, the Welsh word for learner. 'L' or 'D' plates must be fitted to both front and rear of the machine and be clearly visible.

Question
How long is a provisional motorcycle licence valid for?

Mark one answer

● **Two years**
⬭ One year
⬭ Three years
⬭ Five years

A provisional motorcycle licence is valid for two years only. You must take and pass the theory and practical tests within two years or you will have to wait a year before you can apply for another licence. This does not apply if you have a full car or moped licence.

In Northern Ireland provisional licences are valid for ten years.

Question
You are a learner motorcyclist.
The law states that you can carry a passenger when

Mark one answer

● **you have passed your test for a full licence**
○ the motorcycle is no larger than 125cc
○ your pillion passenger is a full licence holder
○ you have had three years' experience of riding

Question
What should you bring with you when taking your driving test?

Mark one answer

● **A signed driving licence**
○ A service record book
○ An insurance certificate
○ An MOT certificate

Question
What should you bring with you when taking your motorcycle test?

Mark two answers

● **A CBT certificate, if you haven't already sent it**
● **A signed driving licence**
○ A service record book
○ An insurance certificate
○ An MOT certificate, if you haven't already sent it

When you are a learner motorcyclist you must comply with certain legal restrictions. The law states you must

• display 'L' (or 'D' in Wales) plates on your machine to front and rear
• not carry pillion passengers
• not use the motorway

When you attend your practical driving test your examiner will ask to see your driving licence. Make sure it is signed or your test may not be conducted.

When you attend a motorcycle test your examiner will ask to see

• your driving licence
• your CBT certificate (except in Northern Ireland)

Make sure your licence is signed and valid or your test may be cancelled. If you have already sent your CBT certificate with your test application the examiner will have a record and not need to see it again.

Question
Before taking a motorcycle test most people need a

NI

Mark one answer
- Compulsory Basic Training (CBT) certificate
- full moped licence
- full car licence
- motorcycle pass certificate

Question
Who MUST you show your driving licence to, on demand?

Mark one answer
- A uniformed police officer
- A third party after an accident
- A vehicle inspector
- A traffic warden

Question
After passing your motorcycle test you must exchange the pass certificate for a full motorcycle licence within

NI

Mark one answer
- two years
- six months
- one year
- five years

Question
For which TWO of these must you show your motor insurance certificate?

Mark two answers
- When a police officer asks you for them
- When you are taxing your vehicle
- When you are taking your driving test
- When buying or selling a vehicle
- When having an MOT inspection

You can find out about a CBT course by asking your motorcycle dealer or by phoning 0115 955 7600.

In Northern Ireland the CBT scheme does not operate so all reference to CBT is not applicable.

Your driving licence is an official document which must be shown to a police officer on demand.

When you pass your practical motorcycle test you will be issued with a pass certificate (Form D.10 – DL8 in Northern Ireland). You must exchange the certificate for a full licence within two years of passing your test. If you don't

- the certificate will lapse
- you will have to retake your test if you wish to resume full motorcycle licence entitlement

When you take out motor insurance you will be issued with a Certificate of Insurance. This contains details explaining who and what is insured. You will have to produce your Certificate of Insurance

- on demand to a police officer
- when you are paying your vehicle excise duty (road tax)

Question
For which TWO of these must you show your motorcycle insurance certificate?

Mark two answers
- **When a police officer asks you for them**
- **When you are taxing your vehicle**
- When you are taking your motorcycle test
- When buying or selling a vehicle
- When having an MOT inspection

Question
A police officer asks to see your driving documents.
You don't have them with you.
You may produce them at a police station within

Mark one answer
- **seven days**
- five days
- 14 days
- 21 days

You don't have to carry your documents with you. If a police officer asks to see them and you don't have them with you, you may produce them at a police station within seven days (five days in Northern Ireland).

Question
Before riding anyone else's motorcycle you should make sure that

Mark one answer
- **the machine is insured for your use**
- the machine owner has third party insurance cover
- your own vehicle has insurance cover
- the owner has the insurance documents with them

If you borrow a motorcycle you must make sure that you are insured. Find out yourself. Don't take anyone else's word for it.

Question
Before driving anyone else's motor vehicle you should make sure that

Mark one answer
- **the vehicle is insured for your use**
- the vehicle owner has third party insurance cover
- your own vehicle has insurance cover
- the owner has left the insurance documents in the vehicle

Before you drive any vehicle on the road make sure that it is insured for your use.

New drivers are considered high risk and this is reflected in high insurance costs. If you are careful and don't have an accident the cost of your insurance will come down, but this is dependent on your occupation.

DSA THEORY TEST for cars and motorcycles

Question
What is the legal minimum insurance cover you must have to drive on public roads?

Mark one answer
- ⬤ **Third party only**
- ◯ Third party, fire and theft
- ◯ Fully comprehensive
- ◯ Personal injury cover

The minimum insurance requirement by law is third party cover. This covers others involved in an accident BUT NOT damage to your vehicle. Basic third party insurance will not cover theft or fire damage. Check with your insurance company for advice on the best cover for you. Make sure you read the policy carefully.

Question
Motorcars and motorcycles must FIRST have an MOT test certificate when they are

Mark one answer
- ⬤ **three years old**
- ◯ one year old
- ◯ five years old
- ◯ seven years old

The vehicle you drive must be in good condition and roadworthy. If it is over three years old it must have a valid MOT test certificate.

In Northern Ireland a vehicle first needs an MOT test certificate when it is four years old.

Question
When is it legal to drive a car over three years old without an MOT certificate?

Mark one answer
- ⬤ **When driving to an appointment at an MOT centre**
- ◯ Up to seven days after the old certificate has run out
- ◯ When driving to an MOT centre to arrange an appointment
- ◯ Just after buying a second-hand car with no MOT

If a vehicle is over three years old it must have a valid MOT certificate if you want to use it on the road. The only time a vehicle is exempt is when it is being driven to an appointment at an MOT testing station.

In Northern Ireland the time limit before an MOT test is needed is four years.

Question
Which THREE of the following do you need before you can drive legally?

Mark three answers
- ⬤ **A valid signed driving licence**
- ⬤ **A valid tax disc displayed on your vehicle**
- ⬤ **A current MOT certificate if the car is over three years old**
- ◯ Proof of your identity
- ◯ Fully comprehensive insurance
- ◯ A vehicle handbook

Before you can drive legally on the road you need

- a signed driving licence
- a current MOT certificate for your vehicle or machine (if it is over three years old or four years in Northern Ireland)
- a current tax disc displayed on your vehicle (unless your vehicle is over 25 years old)

Question
Which THREE of the following do you need before you can ride legally if you don't have a full car licence?

Mark three answers
- ⬤ **A valid signed driving licence**
- ⬤ **A valid tax disc displayed on your vehicle**
- ⬤ **A CBT certificate**
- ◯ Proof of your identity
- ◯ Fully comprehensive insurance
- ◯ A vehicle handbook

If you ride a motorcycle but you don't have a full category B (motor car) licence you will also have to have a CBT certificate (except in Northern Ireland).

In Northern Ireland there is no CBT scheme.

Question
If you do NOT pass your motorcycle test within two years your provisional licence will expire.
You can only apply for another provisional licence after

Mark one answer
- ⬤ **one year**
- ◯ three years
- ◯ six months
- ◯ two years

Provisional motorcycle entitlement on a provisional licence is valid for two years. If you don't pass your motorcycle test within that time the motorcycle entitlement will lapse. You can only apply for renewal of motorcycle entitlement after a period of one year.

This provision does not apply in Northern Ireland.

Question
Which THREE pieces of information are found on a vehicle registration document?

Mark three answers
- ⬤ **Registered keeper**
- ⬤ **Make of vehicle**
- ⬤ **Engine size**
- ◯ Service history details
- ◯ Date of MOT
- ◯ Type of insurance cover

Every vehicle used on the road has a registration document. This is issued by the Driver Vehicle Licensing Agency (DVLA) or the Driver and Vehicle Licensing Northern Ireland (DVLNI) and it keeps a record of the change of ownership. The document states

- date of first registration
- registration number
- previous keeper
- registered keeper
- make of vehicle
- engine size and chassis number
- year of manufacture
- colour

Question
Select TWO answers.
To supervise a leaner driver you MUST

Mark two answers

- ● **have held a full licence for at least three years**
- ● **be at least 21**
- ○ be an approved driving instructor
- ○ hold an advanced driving certificate

Learner drivers must be supervised by a qualified driver who
- has held a full licence for at least three years
- is at least 21 years of age

If you can, learn to drive with a professional. You will be given the correct advice right from the start.

This section looks at what to do in the event of an accident.

The questions will ask you about

- First Aid
- Warning devices
- Reporting procedures
- Safety regulations

Question
You are the first to arrive at the scene of an accident.
Which FOUR of these should you do?

Mark four answers

● Switch off the vehicle engines
● Move uninjured people away from the vehicles
● Call the emergency services
● Warn other traffic
○ Leave as soon as another motorist arrives

Question
You are the first person to arrive at an accident where people are badly injured.
Which THREE should you do?

Mark three answers

● Switch on your own hazard warning lights
● Make sure someone telephones for an ambulance
● Get people who are not injured clear of the scene
○ Try and get people who are injured to drink something
○ Move the people who are injured clear of their vehicles

If you are involved in, or arrive at, the scene of an accident there are actions you should take. It is important to know what to do and also what NOT to do. You could save someone's life, or endanger it.

If you are the first to arrive at the scene of an accident further collisions and fire are the first concerns. You need to

- warn other traffic. Switching on your hazard warning lights will let approaching traffic know there is need for caution
- switch off vehicle engines. This is to reduce the risk of fire
- call or have someone else call the emergency services
- move uninjured people away from the vehicles

Question

You have stopped at the scene of an accident to give help.
Which THREE things should you do?

Mark three answers

● **Keep injured people warm and comfortable**

● **Keep injured people calm by talking to them reassuringly**

● **Make sure injured people are not left alone**

○ Keep injured people on the move by walking them around

○ Give injured people a warm drink

Question

You arrive at the scene of a motorcycle accident. The rider is conscious but in shock.
You should make sure that

Mark one answer

● **the rider's helmet is not removed**

○ the rider's helmet is removed

○ the rider is moved to the side of the road

○ the rider is put in the recovery position

Question

You have an accident and your pillion passenger is injured.
You must NOT

Mark one answer

● **remove their helmet**

○ reassure them

○ keep them in the same position

○ keep them warm

If you stop at the scene of an accident to give help and there are casualties

- reassure injured people and keep them calm
- keep them warm and comfortable
- make sure they are not left alone

Don't

- move injured people, unless further danger is threatened
- give the injured anything to drink

At the scene of a motorcycle accident where a rider or passenger is injured

- don't remove the helmet
- offer reassurance and comfort until the emergency services arrive

Removing a motorcycle helmet could cause further injury. If the rider is conscious reassure them while waiting for the emergency services.

Question

You arrive at the scene of an accident involving a lorry carrying dangerous chemicals.
You stop other vehicles.
What should you do before you dial 999?

Mark one answer

● Find out about the chemicals from labels on the lorry
○ Try to move the lorry
○ Try to dilute the chemicals by washing them away with water
○ Try to stop the chemicals spreading

Question

A tanker is involved in an accident. Which sign would show if the tanker is carrying dangerous goods?

Mark one answer

●

○

○

○

If an accident involves a lorry or tanker it could be carrying hazardous chemicals or dangerous goods. Although there may be no obvious spillage, exposure to air may release poisonous gas.

There will be an orange label on the side and rear of the lorry. Look at this carefully and report what it says when you phone the emergency services.

Question

For which TWO should you use hazard warning lights?

Mark two answers

- ● **When you slow down quickly on a motorway because of a hazard ahead**
- ● **When you have broken down**
- ○ When you wish to stop on double yellow lines
- ○ When you need to park on the pavement

Question

For which THREE should you use your hazard warning lights?

Mark three answers

- ● **When you are temporarily obstructing traffic**
- ● **To warn following traffic of a hazard ahead**
- ● **When you have broken down**
- ○ When you are parking in a restricted area

Question

When are you allowed to use hazard warning lights?

Mark one answer

- ● **When stopped and temporarily obstructing traffic**
- ○ When driving during darkness without headlights
- ○ When parked for shopping on double yellow lines
- ○ When travelling slowly because you are lost

Question

When should you switch on your hazard warning lights?

Mark one answer

- ● **When you cannot avoid causing an obstruction**
- ○ When you are driving slowly due to bad weather
- ○ When you are towing a broken down vehicle
- ○ When you are parked on double yellow lines

Hazard warning lights are fitted to all modern cars and some motorcycles. They should be used to warn other road users of a hazard ahead.

You can use hazard warning lights

- when you have broken down
- when you can't avoid causing an obstruction
- on the motorway when you have to slow down suddenly because of a hazard ahead. This is to warn following traffic that you are slowing suddenly and rapidly

Don't use hazard lights

- to excuse yourself for illegal, dangerous or inconsiderate parking
- when you are moving slowly because you are lost
- when you are moving slowly due to bad weather

DSA THEORY TEST for cars and motorcycles

Question
You have broken down on a two-way road. You have a warning triangle. You should place the warning triangle at least how far from your vehicle?

Mark one answer

● **50 metres (165 feet)**
○ 5 metres (16 feet)
○ 25 metres (80 feet)
○ 100 metres (330 feet)

Question
You are in an accident on an 'A' class road.
At what distance before the obstruction should you place a warning triangle?

Mark one answer

● **50 metres (165 feet)**
○ 100 metres (330 feet)
○ 25 metres (80 feet)
○ 150 metres (495 feet)

Carry an advance warning triangle in your vehicle. They fold flat and don't take up much room. Use it to warn other road users if your vehicle has broken down or there has been an accident. Place your warning triangle

• at least 50 metres (165 feet) from your vehicle on a straight, level road
• at least 150 metres (495 feet) from your vehicle on a dual carriageway or motorway

If there is a bend or hump in the road place the triangle so that approaching traffic slows down before the bend. You must give traffic enough time to react to the warning.

Use your hazard warning lights as well as a warning triangle, especially in the dark.

Question

You have broken down on an ordinary road.
You have a warning triangle. It should be
displayed

Mark one answer

- **at least 50 metres (165 feet) behind your
  vehicle**
- on the roof of your vehicle
- at least 150 metres (495 feet) behind your
  vehicle
- just behind your vehicle

If you need to display a warning triangle
make sure that it can be seen clearly by
other road users. Place it on the same
side of the road and at least 50 metres
(165 feet) from the obstruction.

Question

You have an accident while driving and someone
is injured.
You must report it to the police as soon as
possible, or within

Mark one answer

- **24 hours**
- 48 hours
- five days
- seven days

If you are involved in an accident where
any other person is injured you must

- report it to the police as soon as
  possible, and in any case within
  24 hours
- produce your insurance certificate to
  the police either at the time or
  within seven days

You must also give

- your name and address
- your vehicle owner's address
- the registration number of the
  vehicle

to the police, or anyone with reasonable
grounds for wanting them.

In Northern Ireland accidents have to be
reported to the police 'forthwith'.

DSA THEORY TEST **for cars and motorcycles**

Question
You have an accident and your pillion passenger is injured.
Who must report the accident to the police?

Mark one answer
- ● **You**
- ○ The person who caused the accident
- ○ The injured passenger
- ○ People who witnessed the accident

When you ride a motorcycle you are responsible for your passenger. If you have an accident where your passenger is injured you must tell the police. Don't leave it for someone else to report the accident. It is your responsibility.

Question
At a railway level crossing the red light signal continues to flash after a train has gone by. What should you do?

Mark one answer
- ● **Wait**
- ○ Phone the signal operator
- ○ Alert drivers behind you
- ○ Proceed with caution

When you are waiting at a level crossing and the lights continue to flash after the train has gone by WAIT. Don't

- proceed
- phone the signal operator immediately
- zigzag between the gates

There may be another train coming.

Question
You break down on a level crossing. The lights have not yet begun to flash. Which THREE things should you do?

Mark three answers
- ● **Telephone the signal operator**
- ● **Leave your vehicle and get everyone clear**
- ● **Move the vehicle if a signal operator tells you to**
- ○ Walk down the track and signal the next train
- ○ Tell drivers behind what has happened

If your vehicle breaks down on a level crossing you must

- immediately get everyone out of the vehicle and clear of the crossing
- phone the signal operator
- warn other road users

Don't

- walk up the track to warn approaching trains
- try to restart the engine
- try to move the vehicle

Question
You have stalled in the middle of a level crossing and cannot restart the engine.
The warning bell starts to ring.
You should

Mark one answer
- ● **get out and clear of the crossing**
- ○ run down the track to warn the signalman
- ○ carry on trying to restart the engine
- ○ push the vehicle clear of the crossing

Question
Your vehicle has broken down on an automatic railway level crossing.
What should you do FIRST?

Mark one answer
- ● **Get everyone out of the vehicle and clear of the crossing**
- ○ Phone the signal operator so that trains can be stopped
- ○ Walk along the track to give warning to any approaching trains
- ○ Try to push the vehicle clear of the crossing as soon as possible

Question
Which TWO things should you do when a front tyre bursts?

Mark two answers
- ● **Let the vehicle roll to a stop**
- ● **Grip the steering wheel firmly**
- ○ Change down and brake hard
- ○ Brake firmly and quickly
- ○ Hold the steering wheel lightly

Try not to panic, and stay calm, especially if you have passengers on board. If you can't restart your engine before the warning bells ring then leave the vehicle.

Ensure that everyone is WELL clear of the crossing.

If a tyre bursts while you are driving you will experience some loss of control. If it is a front tyre which bursts keep hold of the steering wheel and stop gradually. Don't

- brake harshly
- release the steering wheel

Motorcyclists should grip the handlebars firmly as a front wheel puncture will cause a lot of shudder.

Question
Your tyre bursts while you are driving.
Which TWO should you do?

Mark two answers

- **Pull up slowly at the side of the road**
- **Hold the steering wheel firmly to keep control**
- Select reverse gear to stop the vehicle
- Give a stopping arm signal and use the gears to slow down
- Stop the vehicle by braking as quickly as possible

Try not to brake harshly and suddenly. Keep calm and stop gradually by the side of the road. You will have some loss of control so keep a balanced hold on the steering wheel.

Question
Your vehicle has a puncture on a motorway. What should you do?

Mark one answer

- **Pull up on the hard shoulder. Use the emergency phone to get assistance**
- Drive slowly to the next service area to get assistance
- Pull up on the hard shoulder. Change the wheel as quickly as possible
- Switch on your hazard lights. Stop in your lane

If you have a puncture when you are travelling on a motorway pull up on the hard shoulder. Make your way to the nearest emergency telephone and request assistance. It may be dangerous to try and change an offside wheel due to fast traffic passing very close to your vehicle.

Question
You use the engine cut-out switch to

Mark one answer

- **stop the engine in an emergency**
- stop the engine for short stops
- save wear on the ignition switch
- start the engine if you lose the key

Most motorcycles are fitted with an engine cut-out switch. This is designed to stop the engine in an emergency and so reduce the risk of fire.

Question

Your vehicle breaks down on a motorway.
You go to the emergency telephone.
Your passengers should

Mark one answer

- ● **wait on the embankment away from the hard shoulder**
- ○ stand next to the vehicle on the hard shoulder
- ○ accompany you to the telephone
- ○ wait inside the vehicle

Question

You are on the motorway.
Luggage falls from your vehicle.
What should you do?

Mark one answer

- ● **Stop at the next emergency telephone and contact the police**
- ○ Stop on the motorway and put on hazard lights whilst you pick it up
- ○ Reverse back up the motorway to pick it up
- ○ Pull up on the hard shoulder and wave traffic down

Question

You are travelling on a motorway.
A bag falls from your motorcycle.
There are valuables in the bag.
What should you do?

Mark one answer

- ● **Stop on the hard shoulder and use the emergency telephone to inform the police**
- ○ Go back carefully and collect the bag as quickly as possible
- ○ Stop wherever you are and pick up the bag, but only when there is a safe gap
- ○ Stop on the hard shoulder and then retrieve the bag yourself

If your vehicle breaks down on the motorway you should try to get over to the hard shoulder. Make your way to the nearest emergency telephone on foot. Marker posts will direct you which way to walk.

If you have any passengers get them to wait on the embankment, away from the hard shoulder. Any pets should stay in the car.

If you are travelling on the motorway and your luggage falls off your vehicle and onto the carriageway you should

- pull over onto the hard shoulder near an emergency telephone
- phone for assistance

Don't

- stop on the carriageway
- attempt to retrieve anything

DSA THEORY TEST for cars and motorcycles

Question
You are driving on a motorway.
A large box falls onto the carriageway from a
lorry ahead of you.
The lorry does not stop.
You should

Mark one answer

● **drive to the next emergency telephone
and inform the police**

○ catch up with the lorry and try to get the
driver's attention

○ stop close to the box and switch on your
hazard warning lights until the police arrive

○ pull over to the hard shoulder, then try and
remove the box

Lorry drivers are sometimes unaware
of objects falling from their vehicles.
If you see something fall off a lorry onto
the motorway watch to see if the driver
pulls over. If the lorry doesn't stop you
should

• pull over onto the hard shoulder
near an emergency telephone
• report the hazard to the police

SECTION 14 VEHICLE LOADING

This section looks at the safety of loads.

The questions will ask you about

- Vehicle loading
- Stability
- Towing regulations

Question
Who is responsible for making sure a vehicle is not overloaded?

Mark one answer

● **The driver or rider of the vehicle**
○ The owner of the items being carried
○ The person who loaded the vehicle
○ The owner of the vehicle

Your vehicle must not be overloaded. This will affect control and handling characteristics. If your vehicle is overloaded and it causes an accident you will be responsible.

Question
Any load that is carried on a luggage rack MUST be

Mark one answer

● **securely fastened when riding**
○ carried only when strictly necessary
○ as light as possible
○ covered with plastic sheeting

Any luggage carried on your vehicle or machine must be secure. It is an offence to travel with an insecure load.

Question
Any load that is carried on a roof rack MUST be

Mark one answer

● **securely fastened when driving**
○ carried only when strictly necessary
○ as light as possible
○ covered with plastic sheeting

If you wish to carry items on the roof there are roof boxes available from motor stores. These will help to keep your luggage secure and dry.

Question
Which THREE are suitable restraints for a child under three years?

Mark three answers

● **A child seat**
● **A harness**
● **A baby carrier**
○ An adult holding a child
○ An adult seat belt
○ A lap belt

The driver is responsible for ensuring that children under three wear suitable child restraints. If the child is in the front seat a restraint **must** be used. If the child is in the rear seat restraints **must** be used if available.

A suitable child restraint for under-three-year-olds could be

- a child seat
- a baby carrier
- a harness or booster seat appropriate to the child's weight

Question

What do child locks in a vehicle do?

Mark one answer

- ⬤ **Stop children from opening rear doors**
- ⬯ Lock the seat belt buckles in place
- ⬯ Lock the rear windows in the up position
- ⬯ Stop the rear seats from tipping forward

Child locks are fitted to most modern cars. They prevent the door being opened from the inside.

Question

Would it be safe to allow children to sit BEHIND the rear seats of a hatchback car?

Mark one answer

- ⬤ **No, not in any circumstances**
- ⬯ Yes, if you can see clearly to the rear
- ⬯ Yes, if they are under 11 years
- ⬯ No, unless all the other seats are full

Children should not be allowed to sit behind the rear seats of a hatchback car. This is a crumple zone and in a rear-end collision the bodywork may intrude into this area.

Question

You should load a trailer so that the weight is

Mark one answer

- ⬤ **evenly distributed**
- ⬯ mostly over the nearside wheel
- ⬯ mainly at the front
- ⬯ mostly at the rear

If you tow a trailer you need to give some thought to how you load it. The load should be

- secured so that it can't move about while you are travelling. Movement of the load might affect steering and cause danger to other road users
- evenly distributed

Question

If a trailer swerves or snakes when you are towing it you should

Mark one answer

- ⬤ **ease off the accelerator and reduce your speed**
- ⬯ let go of the steering wheel and let it correct itself
- ⬯ brake hard and hold the pedal down
- ⬯ increase your speed as quickly as possible

Strong winds or buffeting from large vehicles might cause a trailer or caravan to snake or swerve. If this happens ease off the accelerator. Don't

- brake harshly
- steer sharply
- increase speed

Question

If a trailer swerves or snakes when you are towing it you should

Mark one answer

● **ease off the throttle and reduce your speed**

○ let go of the handlebars and let it correct itself

○ brake hard and hold the brake on

○ increase your speed as quickly as possible

Question

How can you stop a caravan snaking from side to side?

Mark one answer

● **Slow down very gradually**

○ Turn the steering wheel slowly to each side

○ Accelerate to increase your speed

○ Stop as quickly as you can

Question

You have a side-car fitted to your motorbike. What effect will it have?

Mark one answer

● **Increase stopping distance**

○ Reduce stability

○ Make steering lighter

○ Increase fuel economy

Question

Before fitting a side-car riders must

Mark one answer

● **check that their bike is suitable**

○ have the wheels of their bike balanced

○ have their bike's engine tuned

○ pass the extended bike test

Don't be tempted to use the steering to stop swerving or snaking. This will not help the situation. Ease off the throttle and reduce your speed.

If you want to fit a side-car to your motorcycle

• make sure your machine is suitable to cope with the extra load
• make sure the side-car is fixed correctly and properly aligned

A side-car will affect the handling of your machine. Give yourself time to adjust to the different characteristics.

Question
When may a learner motorcyclist carry a pillion passenger?

Mark one answer
- ● **Not at any time**
- ○ If the passenger holds a full licence
- ○ If the rider is undergoing training
- ○ If the passenger is over 21

If you carry a pillion passenger the overall weight of riders and machine will be significantly increased over that when riding alone.

If you are a learner motorcyclist you must not carry a passenger at any time.

Question
Which THREE must a learner motorcyclist under 21 NOT do?

Mark three answers
- ● **Ride a motorcycle with an engine capacity of over 125cc**
- ● **Pull a trailer**
- ● **Carry a pillion passenger**
- ○ Ride faster than 30 mph
- ○ Use the right-hand lane on dual carriageways

If you are a learner motorcyclist under 21 years of age you must not ride a motorcycle on the road with an engine capacity over 125cc.

In Northern Ireland the engine size limit for learners on a motorcycle is 250cc.

Question
Pillion passengers MUST

Mark one answer
- ● **wear a helmet**
- ○ have a provisional motorcycle licence
- ○ be lighter than the rider
- ○ wear reflective or fluorescent clothing

Question
Pillion passengers should

Mark one answer
- ● **lean with the rider when going round bends and corners**
- ○ give the rider directions
- ○ check the road behind for the rider
- ○ give hand signals for the rider

Pillion passengers must

- sit astride the machine facing forward on a proper passenger seat
- wear a safety helmet which is correctly fastened

Pillion passengers should

- lean with the rider when cornering
- keep both feet on the pillion footrests provided

DSA THEORY TEST for cars and motorcycles

Question

To carry a pillion passenger your bike should have which TWO?

Mark two answers

- ⬤ **Rear footrests**
- ⬤ **A proper passenger seat**
- ⬭ An engine of 250cc or over
- ⬭ A top box
- ⬭ A grab handle

Pillion passengers should be instructed not to

- give hand signals
- lean away from the rider when cornering
- fidget or move around
- put their feet down to try and support the machine as you stop
- wear long, loose items which might get caught in the rear wheel or drive chain

This book has been produced to help you to prepare for and pass your theory test. If you have spent sufficient time and effort you will not find the theory question paper difficult.

Passing the theory test is the first stage in becoming a safe driver or rider. Use the knowledge you have learned and put it into practice on the road. You will never know all the answers. Throughout your driving life there will always be more to learn.

The aim of the DSA is to improve road safety throughout the UK. By improving skills and knowledge we can ensure 'Safe Driving for Life'. This will save lives – one of them could be yours.

Service standards for theory test candidates

The DSA and the DVTA are committed to providing the following standards of service for test candidates.

Theory tests will be available

- During weekdays, evenings and on Saturdays. A test appointment should be available for 95% of test candidates within two weeks

- Test notification will be issued within five working days of receipt of a correctly completed application form and appropriate fee

- 95% of telephone calls will be answered within ten seconds

- More time may be needed to make arrangements for candidates with special needs, but a test should be available for 95% of such candidates within four weeks

- Refund of test fees will be issued within three weeks of a valid claim with the supporting information

- All letters to the DSA or the DVTA, including complaints, will be answered within 15 working days

- All candidates should be able to obtain a test booking at their preferred test session within two months of their preferred date and the centre of their choice

- No more than 0.5% of tests will be cancelled by the DSA or the DVTA

Complaints guide for theory test candidates

The DSA and the DVTA aim to give its customers the best possible service. Please tell us

- When we have done well
- When you are not satisfied

Your comments can help us to improve the service we offer. You may be asked to fill out a customer satisfaction questionnaire at the location of your test.

If you have any questions about your theory test please contact Tel: 0645 000 555.

If you are dissatisfied with the reply or you wish to comment on other matters you can write to the office where you booked your test.

If your concern relates to an Approved Driving Instructor, you should write to

The Register of Approved Driving
Instructors
Driving Standards Agency
Stanley House
Talbot Street
Nottingham NG1 5GU

Finally, you can write to

The Chief Executive
Driving Standards Agency
Stanley House
Talbot Street
Nottingham NG1 5GU

None of this removes your right to take your complaint to

- Your Member of Parliament, who can take up your case personally with the DSA Chief Executive, the Minister, or the Parliamentary Commissioner for Administration (the Ombudsman).

The Ombudsman's address is

The Parliamentary Commissioner for
Administration (the Ombudsman)
Church House
Great Smith Street
London SW1P 3BW
Tel: 0171 276 2003/3000

- A magistrates court (in Scotland, to the Sheriff of your area) if you believe that your test was not carried out according to the regulations.

- In Northern Ireland

The Northern Ireland
Parliamentary Commissioner for
Adminstration
Progressive House
33 Wellington Place
Belfast BT1 6HN
Tel: 01232 233 821

Before doing this, you should seek legal advice.

Compensation code for theory test candidates

The DSA will normally refund the test fee, or give a free re-booking, in the following cases

- If we cancel your test

- If you cancel and give us at least three working days' notice

- If you keep the test appointment but the test does not take place or is not finished, for a reason that is not your fault

We will also repay the expenses you incurred on the day of the test because we cancelled your test at short notice. We will consider reasonable claims for

- Travelling to and from the test centre
- Any pay or earnings you lost after tax (usually for half a day)

Please write to the office where you booked your test and send a receipt showing the travel costs and/or an employer's letter which shows what earnings you lost.

The DVTA has a different compensation code. If you think you are entitled to compensation apply to the centre where your test was booked.

This compensation code does not affect your existing legal rights.

DSA THEORY TEST **for cars and motorcycles**

Printed in the United Kingdom for HMSO
Dd 302904 7/96 C800 210035 59226